Sept. '84

To Neil —

Thank you for your interest,
support, and help.

I hope you enjoy reading
· Ultimate Tennis.

Al Secunda

Ultimate Tennis

Al Secunda

Ultimate Tennis

The Pleasure Game

Published in association
with Stan Corwin Productions Ltd.

Prentice-Hall, Inc., Englewood Cliffs, New Jersey 07632

Library of Congress Cataloging in Publication Data

Secunda, Al.
   Ultimate tennis

   Includes index.
   1. Tennis.   2. Tennis—Psychological aspects.
I. Title.
GV995.S365 1984   796.342'019   84-15107
ISBN 0-13-935438-7
ISBN 0-13-935420-4 (Reward book : pbk.)

Book design and layout: Alice R. Mauro
Production coordination: Inkwell
Manufacturing buyer: Pat Mahoney
Cover design by Hal Siegel
Edited by Stephanie E. Bernstein

All pictures and images conceived by Al Secunda.
Art direction by Al Secunda and John Tallman Bissell.
All photographs by John Tallman Bissell except
for the following: Fred Lutz (p. 1, 2-1, 2-2, 2-3, 3-1, 3-3a, 3-3b, 3-3c,
3-4, 3-5a, 3-5b, 9-9 through 9-17b, 10-1, 10-2, 15-1a through 15-1d),
Karen Santillan (5-3a, 5-3b, 5-3c, 6-18a through 6-18e, 7-18a
through 7-18e, 8-17a, 8-17b, 9-7, 9-18, 9-22)
Cover photo by Koji Takei.

This book is available at a special discount when ordered in bulk quantities.
Contact Prentice-Hall, Inc., General Publishing Division, Special Sales,
Englewood Cliffs, N.J. 07632.

10 9 8 7 6 5 4 3 2 1

Prentice-Hall International, Inc., *London*
Prentice-Hall of Australia Pty. Limited, *Sydney*
Prentice-Hall Canada Inc., *Toronto*
Prentice-Hall of India Private Limited, *New Delhi*
Prentice-Hall of Japan, Inc., *Tokyo*
Prentice-Hall of Southeast Asia Pte. Ltd., *Singapore*
Whitehall Books Limited, *Wellington, New Zealand*
Editora Prentice-Hall do Brasil Ltda., *Rio de Janeiro*

ISBN 0-13-935438-7

ISBN 0-13-935420-4 {A REWARD BOOK : PBK.}

This book is dedicated to my loving, generous, and
caring parents, Lou and Bernice Secunda,
who have always believed in me and have always been there
for me regardless of my successes or failures.

Thank you for standing by me
throughout this long and sometimes arduous journey.
I am blessed to be your son.

Contents

Introduction

My story is unusual in that I had never planned to be a professional tennis instructor. Rather, I expected to be a successful businessman who played tennis on the weekends. I never entertained the possibility of playing or teaching full time because tennis never came easily to me. In fact, it was the most difficult and frustrating sport that I ever learned. Although I dreamed of producing graceful and accurate strokes, I had no idea how to create them. This lack of information and technique caused my strokes to remain on a crude and tension-filled level. I became the classic "hacker" who developed a very respectable game only because of many hours of playing. I never understood why my strokes worked when they did work, or how I could get them working again when they were off. You might say that I had reached a sophisticated level of "ignorant proficiency."

In an effort to improve my game, I read many books and studied with many teachers but unfortunately got nowhere. While I was impressed by the literature and by my teachers' strokes, I was never able to *apply* their instruction directly to my game. Out of hopelessness, I finally convinced myself that my impasse was caused by lack of talent.

My game remained on this stagnant and frustrating level until I left the business world to pursue the performing arts. To my amazement, I quickly discovered that tennis and the performing arts were extremely similar. In fact, I began to view tennis as an art form. With this revelation, the barriers to my game slowly started to disappear. I began to develop a new approach to understanding tennis. At the same time, my strokes became graceful, accurate, and consistent beyond my wildest dreams.

As my game was being transformed, I realized that the process I was developing represented an entirely new system of learning the game. I became so excited that I began to teach. I suppose you could say that I became a tennis missionary. Much to my delight, this revolutionary learning process was also of great help to my students. They too began to develop a new understanding of the entire sport, regardless of their level of play. Through this transformation they experienced new dedication, commitment, and excitement.

The feedback from my students was so positive and supportive that I decided to make this information available to more of the tennis world. I knew that to do this I would have to create a unique and practical tennis book, one from which people *could actually learn tennis.* What you are about to read is the culmination of this endeavor.

The purpose of *Ultimate Tennis: The Pleasure Game* is to help you to improve your game while having fun. Learning tennis need not be a tedious or painful experience. The unique pictures, vocabulary, and text are all designed to allow you to learn while having an enjoyable experience.

The book basically revolves around two words: *pleasure* and *precision.* Each time the strings *properly* meet the ball, an extremely pleasurable vibration is created throughout the entire body. It should *feel good* to produce a tennis stroke, regardless of the results. When this enjoyable experience produces a precise result—the ball flies over the net and lands where you intended it to—you have created the ultimate tennis stroke. The purpose of this book is to help you improve the physical enjoyment and the accuracy of each stroke.

This book will also encourage you to *play* more upon entering a tennis court. Most tennis players have unfortunately forgotten the meaning of the word *play.* When we were young we knew what it meant to be a "player." We'd play in the sandbox. We'd make up games and play them with our friends. Playing was a pleasurable experience. Unfortunately, what most of us are doing on the court is not "playing." We are "seriousing." "John is out seriousing at tennis. He'll be back at two." The problem with seriousing is that it is not fun, and the body does not function at its optimum athletic level when we are in a serious and/or tense state. The material in this book was created to help you to play more at tennis. "Playing" will improve the pleasure and precision of your strokes.

I feel blessed for having been given a second chance at understanding and playing tennis. Now you have a second chance as well. For those of you who have thought about playing tennis ho have struggled with it for many years, this is your golden opportunity to finally improve your game. If your game has been stagnating—or if you have been afraid even to begin learning the sport—what you have lacked is insight, not talent. It is my sincere belief that with the new information contained in this book, you will ultimately be able to first recognize and then realize your true tennis potential.

Acknowledgments

I was most influenced by three master teachers, Peter Burwash, Joseph K. Scott, and Tad Danielewski. Their theories and philosophies (in tennis and the performing arts) helped to form the foundation for this new and unique system of learning tennis.

Peter Burwash is president of Peter Burwash International, an international group of tennis teachers. Peter's teachings helped me to realize the importance of the moment of contact between the ball and strings. He also helped me to understand that power should be the last ingredient added to a stroke. His dedication to tennis and to the teaching process worldwide is unparalled. Peter has supported and encouraged my creativity as both a person and a tennis teacher.

Joe Scott is a loving and profound singing coach living in Manhattan. Joe taught me that singing is a feeling rather than a listening experience. Through him I learned to focus my attention on creating and experiencing the note, rather than on listening and worrying about the results of that note. This philosophy enabled my singing to become more enjoyable, expressive, and precise.

When I applied Joe's principle on the tennis court, my game improved dramatically. I realized that most players are at the moment of contact too concerned about the results of their stroke—where the ball is going to land. This "result orientation" usually minimizes the total physical experience and jeopardizes the precision of the stroke. Therefore, the body's first priority when producing a tennis stroke should always be pleasure and comfort. The precision should be born out of a pleasurable stroking experience.

Tad Danielewski is an articulate, insightful, and inspirational film and television director who taught me that the more specific the "action" of the performer, the more precise the results.

Tad also taught me the importance of keeping the body free of tension whenever these specific actions are being produced. Unnecessary body tension can sabotage the entire performance. I soon saw that the strokes of most tennis players are also an unsuccessful compilation of generalized tense actions. Instead, a tennis stroke should be made up of a series of specific actions so that specific and consistent results can be achieved. While performing these specific actions, the body should be in a relaxed and tension-free state.

EXTRA-SPECIAL THANKS TO:

Stephanie E. Bernstein, editor, for her friendship, dedication, wisdom, and love. More than any other person she helped to shape, mold, and organize this book; *Jules Buccieri* for his guidance, love, and friendship, and for helping me to make Los Angeles my new home; *Louis Cohen* for his early editorial comments, which went far beyond the call of duty; *Stan Corwin* for believing in me and my teaching method and for helping to make this book a reality; special thanks to *Ken, Judy,* and *Meredith Davis, Terry Deck, Bob Gold, Pete Hammer, Alan Hecht, Neil Levine,* and *Jay Lubinsky* for their support and long-time friendship; *Nick D'Incecco* for recognizing the validity of my teaching method and for helping to maintain the book's educational and artistic integrity; *Mr. and Mrs. Mel Dorfman* for the use of their magnificent tennis court; special thanks to *Michael Gottsegen* for his assistance, new friendship, and great tennis successes during the Pan American Maccabiah Games; *Stephen Johnson* for his support, concern, and love for me during this project; *Cliff, Lee, Mark, and Ian Harris* for opening their hearts and home to me and for making me feel like a member of the family; *John Holsinger* for being a great tennis teacher and for helping me to realize my potential as a teacher; *Marvin, Fran and Loren Kaplan* for their friendship, support, help, and love; *Isgo Lepejian* for his professional expertise and personal interest in the development and printing of these pictures; *Ken Lo* for his artistic skills and for his dedication to this project; *Sergio Premoli* for his constant encouragement, support, and love; *Richard Ritz* for being my most improved student; *Mario Sanchez* for all of his help, interest, and time; *Larry Schonbrun Esq.* for his help, enthusiasm, and love, and for his growth and development into a fine tennis player; *Michael Smollins* for his friendship, love and assistance; *Valerie Spitzer* for her fantastic retouching work; *John Tallman* for his fantastic photographs, support, and dedication to this project; and to *Judy Secunda William* for her constant help and love and for being my wonderful and special sister.

Finally, I would be remiss if I didn't extend my special thanks to the following: "Doc" Adams, Rosa Aguirre, Nick and Nancy Bahouth, David and Angela Bailey, Jack Banner, Ethel Bernard, Myron Blatt, Cisco Brushman, Johnny Butler, Lori Butler, Richard Calo, Fred Claire, Jim Clinch, Paul Cohn, Tom and Judy Conel, Jan Cox, Corky Cramer, Gene Czaplinsky, Fred Dahl, Stephen Dart, David DeGeus, Joe Dinoffer, Roger Duval, Carl Earn, Ben and Anne Efraim, FILA, Millard Fillmore, Sal Gamboa, Silvana Gallardo, the Geldon family—Earl, Ruth, Fred and Gil, Chuck and Dottie Gibson, Dan Gilbert, Dr. Andrew Goldberg, Larry Goldman, Michael Gottsegen, Berry Gordy, Jeff Green, Steve Greene, Seymour Griss, Bernard Gusman, Bruce Haase, Steve Halverson, Peter Hammer, Skip Hartman, Peggy Hehman, Michael Henry, Janet Himelstein, Steve Hoffman, Barb Horton, Jon Hutner, Jerome Jann, Fran Johnson, Bill Jordan, Kaepa Shoes, Herb Karp, Moe and Kathy Keating, Adrian Lambert, David Lane, Johnny Lane, Judith Lang, Carol Lefcourt, the Leifer family—Wally, Helen, and Lorin, Anoush Lepejian, Barett Lepejian, Dr. Ed Lew, P. Liebowitz, Suzanne de Passe Lumet, Fred Lutz, Lorne McFadgen, Fred "Doc" Marston, Don Martinetti, Chris Massetani, M.J. Novotny Merriman, Charles J. Millevoi, Pamela Mishlove, Hank Muckerman, Jody Myers, Ted Murray, Swami Muktananda, Harriet Neimer, Ron Nolte, Judy Nyren, Ed Palmer, Janice Larson Parry, Bernard Percy, Laura Prizant, Pro Kennex, Jim Pyle, Rafi's Market, Bill Reed, Chris Reid, Bill Rombeau, Jack Rosenberg, Karen Santillan, Barry and Penny Secunda, the Sheingold family—Harry, Helen, Joan, and Carl, David Sigal, Inez Spalding, Koji Takei, Chris Alati Varjian, Jay Wanderman, Kris Wakeford, Gina Warwick, Bob Waunch, Gene Weiss, Jim Witter, the William family—Larry, Judy, Paul, and Lisa, Ben and Sheila Wise and Fiona Wong.

How to Use This Book

1. This book was written for the beginner as well as the advanced player. The entertaining nature of some of the pictures was designed to make the learning process more pleasurable and memorable. The advanced player who incorrectly thinks that these pictures were created just for the beginner is missing a rare opportunity to improve his or her game. The more advanced the player, the more these pictures should be studied.

2. This book was designed to be read and re-read. You will not be able to digest all of this material in just one reading. The more times that you re-read (or refer to) this material, the more new insights you will keep discovering. In fact, you will find this book most helpful if you read only one or two chapters per day (or even per week). Each chapter should be read slowly and thoroughly to give you time to absorb the information intellectually, emotionally, and physically. By reading the book in this fashion, it will become more of a total learning experience.

3. In this book you will be introduced to many new tennis "actions." In order for these new actions to feel natural and comfortable, they must be practiced. When practicing them, do the following:

    a. Regardless of how advanced you are, practice only one action at a time. Do not combine actions. Each action can be learned faster when practiced individually and slowly.

    b. Focus all of your attention on producing the correct physical action. Never think or worry about the results of that action (where the ball is going). It is very difficult to produce new actions when you are simultaneously demanding successful results. This "result-oriented syndrome" usually prevents the player from ever learning the correct action in its pure form.

    c. Make sure that your body is in a comfortable and relaxed state when you are producing these new actions.

4. Every now and then an approaching ball will cause an "emergency situation" that might prevent you from using the specific actions introduced in this book. Abandon these actions only as a last resort. Remember to return to them on the very next shot.

5. The English language is constructed with a bias toward the male pronoun *he*. Throughout this book *he* will refer to both men and women. Unfortunately, we are not programmed enough to accept the pronoun *she* as also referring to both men and women.

6. The most unique aspect of this book is that it deals more with what a correct stroke should feel like rather than the exact physical reality of stroke production (what a camera would actually show). This feeling concept is transferred to you through simulated stop-action photographs. Therefore, you should not try to copy my exact tennis form. Rather, use these pictures to gain a new understanding of how each element of a stroke should feel.

Ultimate Tennis

chapter 1

Pleasure and Precision

This chapter was designed to introduce you to the two basic elements of tennis mastery described in this book: *PLEASURE AND PRECISION*.

Most tennis books emphasize technique over enjoyment, power over finesse—and here is where *Ultimate Tennis* is radically different. I believe that precision is only 50 percent of the game. Obviously it is a very important 50 percent—but it is no more than that. The purpose of this book, then, is to acquaint the player, whether beginner or advanced, with the other 50 percent of the sport—pleasure. For out of pleasure comes additional precision; the body is most efficient at performing when it is in a relaxed and receptive state.

To help you readily understand how the concepts of pleasure and precision are used throughout this book, this chapter will define those important terms and give you some valuable information to help you assimilate these principles into your tennis game. After you have worked with this material, you will be ready to get into the specifics of the pleasure and precision program, geared toward helping you experience, through pictures, exercises, and images, how ultimate tennis strokes should feel when they are performed correctly.

> *Man's mind, stretched to a new idea, never goes back to its original dimension.*
> Oliver Wendell Holmes

ULTIMATE TENNIS: THE PLEASURE GAME

People who have mastered any sport, skill, craft, or art form have successfully learned how to combine two elements: pleasure and precision. What makes a great performance is more than the precise execution of certain movements. It is the joy and seeming effortlessness expressed by the player as he or she successfully executes specific actions. This is just as true for the basketball player as for the concert pianist.

In tennis the body can be relaxed and comfortable while creating an accurate stroke. This is the ultimate tennis stroke: The stroke feels good to produce *and* goes where you want it to go, time and time again. Unfortunately, most players go through life never able to produce Ultimate Tennis Strokes. Either their shots are precise—causing tension, strain, and sometimes even tennis elbow—or they are pleasurable and imprecise—flying over the fence or into the net.

Although most players have the ability to combine pleasure and precision, they do not make use of their ability. Generally, accuracy is valued more than enjoyment, caused by what I believe is a misplaced "precision priority." This precision priority falsely leads players to think that tension helps control the shot. What they don't realize is that a stroke works *in spite of tension*, not because of it. If they are the least bit competitive, they will never want to eliminate the tension for fear of losing control. They therefore never give themselves a chance to experience the pure physical enjoyment of a properly executed stroke.[1]

People who have mastered tennis, however, never have to choose between pleasure and precision. Rather, they combine both ingredients each time they produce a tennis stroke. Pleasure is built into their precise stroking technique.

Although it might seem otherwise, the shortcut to learning an Ultimate Tennis Stroke is for pleasure to take priority over precision. The body will be able to execute and absorb specific physical actions much sooner when you are in a relaxed and comfortable state. Doing the correct repetitions in a "pleasure priority" environment will enable you to learn with fewer practice repetitions. The body will eventually find its own control (precision) through comfort and precise actions.

1. Ethel Bernard, President of Pain Management Group of Long Beach and Culver City, once mentioned to a patient the importance of freeing the body of tension. "What are you talking about?" responded the patient. "My tension is the only thing holding my body and life together."

Opposite page: Figure 1-1
We should never forget the most important principle of tennis—*to have fun.*
(A player who has forgotten this principle).

PLEASURE

In this chapter pleasure will be discussed in terms of three areas: pleasure on the court, pleasure stroking a ball, and pleasure at moment of contact.

Pleasure on the Court

The entire experience of being on the court should be fun. Even the act of picking up a tennis ball or chasing a ball that flew over the fence should be an enjoyable and energizing experience.

Pleasure Stroking a Ball

Producing a stroke should be a nurturing and therapeutic experience for the entire body (especially the shoulder and arm).

Pleasure at Moment of Contact

Your body has the potential to experience the most enjoyment at moment of contact. This enjoyable vibration, however, can only be realized when the body (especially the shoulder and arm) is in a relaxed and comfortable state. Only the absence of tension will allow your body to fully experience the moment of contact.

PLEASURE ON THE COURT

> *While precision is of major importance, the continuous pleasure of a performer is still more important than any given mistake that might occur.*

Your Body Is the Creator and the Audience

Recently I was playing a very enjoyable competitive match. Some time during the second set, however, I spotted several heads looking out of an office building window that was overlooking the courts. As each point progressed, I became more and more self-conscious. As I became more aware of my audience, I began to remove myself from the experience of actually feeling and creating each stroke. Suddenly, my game began to fall apart. Pleasing the audience became more important than pleasing myself.

Just before starting to serve the next game, I decided to take a quick peek up at the window to see clearly who these people were. As my eyes focused in on the window, I became extremely embarrassed. My audience turned out to be three flower pots.

Anyone who ever watches you play tennis must be thought of as a flower pot. Flower pots don't count and neither do the people watching you.

YOU MUST FIRST PHYSICALLY PLEASE YOURSELF BEFORE ANYONE ELSE CAN BE SATISFIED.

Go Swimming on a Tennis Court

When you are hot and uncomfortable, going for a swim can be a delightful and refreshing experience. While in the water, you are not trying to perfect your swimming strokes; rather, you are trying to experience some enjoyment. The purpose of being in the water is *pleasure*, not perfection.

Similarly, the main purpose of being on a tennis court should always be to experience enjoyment. Yet, when we enter a tennis court, we usually first demand precision from our strokes. This priority should be reversed. Upon entering the court put yourself into a "pleasure trance." While in this trance, you can experience pleasure from such mundane actions as stretching, opening a can of tennis balls, taking your racket cover off, etc.

There are 3,600 seconds in an hour. Each second represents a potentially enjoyable moment. Therefore, if you are playing tennis for an hour, you have 3,600 opportunities to bathe in comfort. Take advantage of as many of these moments as possible.

Snapping Back

Always try to have a pleasurable and energized experience from the time you enter the tennis court until you leave it, regardless of whether you are playing well or not. Having an enjoyable and energizing experience creates the proper environment for one of two things to happen:

1. It will allow you to enter the court and play better tennis.
2. It will allow you to "snap back" and play better tennis whenever your game is off.

I know it is difficult to have fun when you are playing poorly, but this is the short-cut to snapping back and playing well. This skill is probably the most important (and difficult) competitive tool to develop.

At the end of each point, be aware of whether or not you are in a pleasurable and energized state. Then use the mental and physical techniques presented in this book to help you remain in or return to this enjoyable state.

PLEASURE STROKING A BALL

> *A tennis ball will sometimes go over the net and into the opponent's court in spite of tension not because of it.*

Stroke Fluidity

The fluidity of a tennis stroke is very similar to the fluidity of water. Like the flow of water, the stroke should be smooth, continuous, gentle, and caressing. The forward momentum of the racket should never be abruptly stopped. Rather than prematurely stopping a stroke with tension and muscle, you should allow the racket and arm to flow and coast into a full and enjoyable completion.

Moving the hand forward through water in a swimming pool (or bathtub) closely simulates the correct *stroke fluidity sensation*. (See Figure 1–2.)

During the entire forward motion of the tennis stroke the strings should feel as if they were *floating forward*. Try to imagine that the strings are floating forward because they are being supported by a rubber tube. The right arm and shoulder do not have to do any work to keep the strings from sinking. (See Figure 1–3.)

Greater Than Five

Creating a tennis stroke should be an extremely enjoyable experience. In fact, it should feel better producing the stroke than not producing it. Here is a little exercise to determine whether producing the stroke is in fact a pleasurable experience.

While waiting for your opponent to return the ball, become aware of what state your

Figure 1-2
Moving the hand forward through water in a swimming pool (or bathtub) closely simulates the correct *stroke fluidity sensation.*

body is in. Let's call this state a 5. A 1 state would be very tense, a 5 state would be relaxed and comfortable, and a 10 state would be highly pleasurable.

Your goal when producing each stroke is to have the body experience states from 6 to 10.

If you are producing strokes that are placing your body in states less than 5, you are trying to achieve precision through tension and muscle, rather than precision through an enjoyable physical experience.

Your ultimate goal as a player is to receive 10s while having precise strokes.

Pleasuring a Winner

Have you ever noticed how many errors you produce whenever you try to hit "a winner"? Let me suggest to you one possible reason: Your body is trying to produce the winning shot by using power, muscle, or tension. At moment of contact with the ball, your shoulder and arm are in a tense, aggressive state.

Rather than trying to muscle a winner, you should try to *pleasure a winner*. Let the entire body (especially the arm and shoulder) be in ecstasy throughout an offensive, winning shot. Your goal when stroking a winner is to *please your body first*. Always have this as your first priority.

Breathing

Often our breathing patterns inadvertently contribute to the amount of tension we have in our bodies. For example, holding one's breath during a stroke tends to promote body rigidity, leading to pleasureless stroking. Here is a technique that will enable you to become less tense when stroking the ball. During a tennis stroke, the player should be receiving pleasure and inhaling air at the same time. He should "drink in" the air just as he "drinks in" the pleasure that each stroke produces. Breathing will produce pleasurable sensations throughout the body.

Just as you are about to contact the ball, start to inhale slowly and continue to inhale during the entire tennis stroke. (Exhaling during a stroke is sometimes counterproductive because it tends to promote too much muscular power and/or tension. If you prefer to exhale, then at least exhale with a slow, gentle, and pleasurable stream of air.)

When a player inhales with a steady, soothing rhythm and gets pleasure from his stroke, he often feels so relaxed that he may correlate this freedom from tension with lack of control. Stay with this new feeling of pleasure and freedom. Ultimately, control will be born from this new feeling. *Tension is not control. Control is a by-product of pleasure.*

The $10,000 Racket

Try not to work too hard when creating a tennis stroke. Let the racket do more of the work. We must trust the racket as if it had strength, wisdom and a life of its own.

Figure 1-3
Imagine that the strings are floating forward.

Figure 1-4
Try to become this relaxed at moment of contact.

Imagine that you have just bought a $10,000 racket. The only reason that you would ever spend this kind of money is that the salesperson told you that the racket would play tennis for you. All you have to do is to hold it and start the racket on its way forward.

Now if you took this expensive racket onto the court and started to use a lot of power, tension, and muscle to create your strokes, you would never know whether or not the salesperson took you for a lot of money. So, regardless of what kind of racket you own, treat it like a $10,000 racket. See how much work you can get it to do. As your game improves, you will do less and the racket will do more. *The more*

work the racket does, the more pleasure you will receive.

PLEASURE AT MOMENT OF CONTACT

At moment of contact with the ball the body should embrace rather than brace.

The Sensation of Contacting a Ball

In Hawaii, Peter Burwash International teaches the blind how to stroke a tennis ball. Blind players come back week after week for this free class. They can't return the ball that someone else hits, but they can and do learn how to bounce the ball and stroke it with the racket. Now, if the blind cannot see their results, why do they come back? The answer is because each stroke *feels so good.* One could hear them shout "That was a good one," and "That was a bad one." A good and bad what? Good and bad feelings, sensations, and vibrations. One shot pleased the body and one did not. That's the main measure of success and failure.

STROKING A TENNIS BALL IS A PLEASURABLE EXPERIENCE.

> *Feel the results before you see the results.*

Surrender

When you take a jacuzzi or hot bath notice how relaxed your body becomes after a few moments in the water. While in this "open" state, your body "surrenders" to the water. Likewise, when your racket meets the ball, your entire body (especially your shoulder and arm) should be in a similar state. In order to experience the most pleasure from a tennis stroke, at moment of contact your body should be in an "open," comfortable, and relaxed state. (See Figure 1–4.) Rather than "holding on," your body must learn how to "let go."

The Racket Should Coast into Contact with the Ball

Most of your work should be done *before* contact occurs. At moment of contact the racket has a force of its own. As the strings meet the ball, the racket does most of the work, and you should be mainly vacationing. *The racket should feel as though it were coasting into contact* rather than accelerating into contact. If at moment of contact the racket accelerates too abruptly, you risk creating a tension-filled, imprecise stroke. Remember, whenever you work too hard, you jeopardize pleasure and precision.

AT MOMENT OF CONTACT, THE RACKET SHOULD GIVE AS YOU RECEIVE.

TENSION

Tension usually prevents players from ever realizing a pleasurable tennis stroke. There are two major types of tension: tension induced by trying to muscle, over-power, and/or control the ball, and the tension induced by fear.

Physical Tension

Too many players have physical tension in their neck, shoulder, and arm when contacting the ball. This type of tension is a major cause of tennis elbow. The arm produces a motion that is stressful, painful, and non-nurturing to the body, just for the sake of "control." Below are two examples of what I mean by physical tension.

1. Raise your right shoulder up to your ear. Leave it in this position for ten seconds. This is physical tension.
2. Bend your right arm to its maximum and clench your fist as tightly as possible. This is also physical tension.

At moment of contact, the neck, shoulder, and arm should be in a relaxed and comfortable state while being free of physical tension.

Mental Tension

This type of tension is induced by fear: You get in a tournament above your head; you're the fourth in a doubles game when you should be the ball boy; you're playing your fiance's mother and she's slaughtering you. All these circumstances—and no doubt many others—create anxiety that in turn manifests as tension in the body.

This section contains several techniques to help alleviate both types of tension.

Residual Shoulder and Arm Tension

A tennis player is very susceptible to tension. First, tension will enter the body just because tennis is a competitive sport. Second, producing a tennis stroke tends to produce shoulder and arm tension. This tension tends to remain and to build up as one continually takes more and more strokes. I call this *residual tension*, tension that the body should be freed of as soon as it appears.

Tension stifles our potential to produce a pleasurable and precise stroke.

After completing a tennis stroke, try to relax the *shoulder, arm,* and *hand* while wait-

Figure 1-5
The incorrect facial expression and shoulder position.

ing for your opponent to return each ball. It is crucial that the shoulder and arm be permitted to return to a relaxed and comfortable position before each new stroke is created.

The Light Bulb Test

One way to determine your tension level is to picture your body covered with millions of very small light bulbs. As long as your body stays free, comfortable, and relaxed, all the little bulbs will stay off. However, if there is tension anywhere in your body, the bulbs will light up in those tense areas. Raise your right shoulder and try to press it against your ear. Notice what areas of your body would light up. The shoulder, neck, and part of the back are most likely to do so. Now release the shoulder and let it fall limply. All the light bulbs will go off.

While on a tennis court, your goal should be to create consistent and accurate tennis strokes while keeping all of the light bulbs off.

(This is especially important in competition.) The more aggressive your opponent's shots are, the greater your dedication must be to producing strokes without any lights.

Because you must hold onto the racket, it is permissible to have the light bulbs on in the hand at the moment of contact.

A Pleasurable Facial Expression and Shoulder

At moment of contact, your face and shoulder should be in a relaxed and comfortable state. Tension interferes with pleasure and precision. (See Figure 1–5.)

To help reduce body tension do one of the following:

1. Gently inhale (or exhale) at moment of contact.
2. Relax your jaw and produce a *yawn* at moment of contact.

Both of the above actions will help alleviate most body and facial tension when contacting the ball.

Practicing a Pleasurable Stroke

The safest place to practice and experience pleasurable strokes is in a noncompetitive environment. Competition tends to breed tension. Therefore, create safe and enjoyable practicing situations for yourself. When playing, rally more.[2] Don't play so many sets of tennis. A noncompetitive environment will encourage you to risk more.

Remember that when a ball approaches at

---

2. Rally—to stroke the ball back and forth over the net without officially keeping score.

a fast pace, it will tend to cause you to produce a tense stroke. Therefore, do the following:

1. When using a ball machine, set the speed of the ball at a fairly slow pace.
2. When using a backboard, stroke the ball slowly.

PRECISION

> POWER *corrupts in politics—and tennis.*

Consistency

Consistency is an important element of precision. Your tennis stroke must repeatedly send the ball *over* the net and *into* the desired area of your opponent's court.

Figure 1-6
Shooting pool and playing tennis are similar skills.

The precision of a tennis player is similar to the precision of an assembly line worker. Both individuals must *consistently* perform specific actions time after time. If the precision actions are not consistently performed, the tennis player loses the point, and the assembly line worker loses a job.

Power

I don't know how to break this to you, but tennis is *not* a power sport. In fact, the more power you add to your strokes, the less likely it is that you will ever develop a consistent game. Now there is nothing wrong with a powerful and inconsistent game. In fact, the act of smashing each ball can be a wonderful way to release an enormous amount of physical and mental aggression. The problem arises, however, when you also expect precision and consistency from these wildly aggressive strokes. You must either be a brilliant athlete or have developed a highly sophisticated stroking technique in order to combine power with precision and consistency. The faster the racket moves, the more likely it is that your precision will be compromised. Power increases the chances of producing an inconsistent stroke. The height of the net and limited size of a tennis court make it essential that power be the *last* ingredient to be added to a tennis stroke.

When and if you do decide to add power, make sure it comes from relaxation and comfort, rather than muscle and tension.

Balance

Unless the body is balanced *throughout* the tennis stroke, consistent precision is very difficult. The easiest way to achieve balance is to keep your feet stationary and fairly wide apart before, during, and after moment of contact. If you cannot always remain stationary, then at least keep the body well balanced when in motion. All professional "performers" make their skills appear to be easy because they always remain well balanced.

Concentration

The precision of a stroke is usually compromised whenever we simultaneously become the player and the critic. As "precision performers" we must learn to always please ourselves before we please anyone else. The following story deals with these points.

While working at the Sheraton-Town House, in Los Angeles, I had an opportunity to give a tennis lesson to Naoki, a gentleman from Japan. He was a karate teacher and a top competitor in Japan. Toward the end of the first lesson, we played a set of tennis. I beat him 6–1, but I worked much harder than the score indicates. I was shocked to learn that he had been playing tennis only for a year. How could he have become so good? I noticed that whenever he contacted the ball his concentration was intense. Maybe he was able to apply his karate concentration to tennis. After the lesson, I asked, "When you break bricks with your hands, what do you think about when your hand contacts the bricks?" His answer gave me a great insight into both karate and tennis.

Naoki's technique revolves around a concept of believing. He tells himself a short story and *totally believes* it. If he fails to believe the story, he will injure himself. As Naoki's hand makes contact with the bricks, he truly believes that he *dies*. He never worries about his success or failure at breaking the bricks, because he is never present to see the results. That is, he picks a specific point on the top brick and *totally disappears* at moment of contact *within the bricks*. His momentary death is a freeing and ecstatic experience, not a painful one. This technique allows him to fully experience the moment of contact.

Once, photographers were going to take pictures of him breaking bricks. As they gathered around him with their cameras, Naoki became too concerned with impressing them and not concerned enough with his own preparation. "When I contacted the bricks, I no die," he said. He wound up in the hospital with a broken hand.

Using Naoki's technique on a tennis court will help your tennis game. One of the secrets of tennis is to *experience totally the moment of contact* and not to worry about the results of the stroke. Fully experiencing the moment of contact will help you to achieve a pleasurable and precise tennis stroke.

Diamond Cutting

It is helpful to correlate tennis with diamond cutting. A diamond cutter knows the importance of remaining balanced and stationary. He also understands that he will probably compromise his precision if he raises the hammer too far above the chisel.

Tennis is similar to diamond cutting in the following ways:

> Keeping the body stationary and balanced will improve the precision of a stroke.
>
> Shortening the backswing (the distance the racket travels backwards) will also enhance the precision of a stroke.

Remember that even though a tennis racket is a fairly large instrument, moment of contact is still a precise, specific, and exact experience.

Shooting Pool

Shooting pool and playing tennis are both very similar. (See Figure 1–6.) They both require finesse, not power. Following is a list that contains additional similarities:

1. You should achieve precision through eliminating excess body motion. With less body motion the shoulder, arm, and hand are more likely to achieve precision.
2. You should be totally balanced when contacting the ball.
3. You should line up the ball properly.

SUMMARY

Pleasure

> Try to enjoy every second you are on the court.
>
> Producing the entire tennis stroke should be a pleasurable experience.
>
> Your body should experience the most enjoyment at moment of contact.
>
> Control and power are by-products of pleasure.

Precision

> Power tends to compromise precision.
>
> At the moment of contact, try to keep the body well balanced and stationary.
>
> Concentration helps the precision of a stroke.

Note: The Learning Process is also a very important chapter. Although it appears later in the book, I strongly recommend that it be read at your earliest possible convenience.

Two Constants
and Two
Variables

> *There are some things which can not be learned easily (quickly)—they are the very simplest things, and because it takes a man's life to know them, the little each man gets is very costly and the only heritage he has to leave.*
>
> —*Ernest Hemingway*

This chapter deals with a new way of looking at tennis. This approach is just as valid for the tournament player as it is for the beginner. In fact, the more advanced the player, the more important this information becomes.

We can sum up this chapter in two statements:

1. Tennis is a game of two constants (the net and court) and two variables (the ball and racket).

2. The racket must contact the ball in such a way as to send it *over* the *net* and *into* the opponent's *court*.

This entire book is, in one sense, an explanation of the above two points. Whenever a beginning player wants to learn tennis, or an advanced player wants to dig out of a rut and climb up to the next plateau, it is vital that he returns to these basics. The player (regardless of his current tennis level) who takes his time to read and digest this chapter will get the most out of the succeeding chapters.

CONSTANT ONE

The Net

The tennis net is the first constant. (See Figure 2–1.) It is a high stationary wall disguised as a low wall. A tennis player thinks that the net is lower than it is because he can see through it. In fact, the tennis net is a very high obstacle, and the player must not be fooled by this optical illusion. The net is three feet high in the middle and it grows to three and a half feet as it approaches the net post.

CONSTANT TWO

The Court

The tennis court is the second constant. It is divided in half by the net. Your opponent's half of the court becomes your target.

Figure 2-1
The tennis net is the first constant.

The net is so high that if it were covered, and if you were standing on the baseline, you would not be able to see the lines on your opponent's court (your target).(See Figure 2–2).

For a detailed diagram containing the parts and dimensions of a tennis court turn to page 226.

VARIABLE ONE: THE BALL

The tennis ball is the first variable. It is made of rubber, covered with cloth. The rubber helps you to produce a stroke with power, and the cloth covering helps you to produce a stroke with spin.

VARIABLE TWO: THE RACKET

The racket is the second variable. Tennis rackets come in many sizes and shapes. The strings of the racket are referred to as the *face* of the racket.

WHY YOUR OPPONENT IS NOT A VARIABLE

Many tennis teachers consider the opponent to be an important variable. This is a good concept in theory, but in practice it can cause more problems than it solves. The majority of players

Figure 2-2
The tennis court is the second constant.

Diagram 2-1
The arc of a tennis ball.

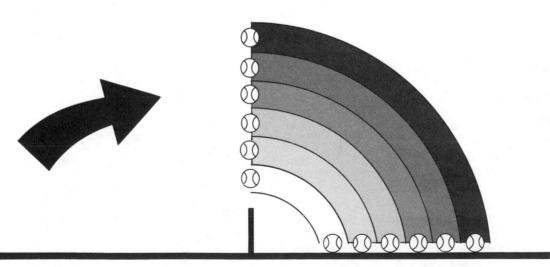

lose points as a result of their own errors, not because of an opponent's superior game. In fact, many errors occur simply because at moment of contact, players are concentrating too much on their opponent, and not enough on contacting the ball.

Don't worry so much about your opponent. Even when you are not concentrating directly on him, your peripheral vision will usually tell you where he is. When you become a more advanced player, your opponent can become a more important variable, but until then, concentrate more on the ball, the strings, and your stroke.

THE "OVER AND IN" CONCEPT

The importance of thinking about the net as an obstacle and the opponent's court as a target area cannot be overstated. This is a universal principle that is just as valid for the tournament player as it is for the beginner.

Stated very simply, tennis is a game of "OVER AND IN."

"Over"

A tennis player's *first physical priority* is to program the ball to fly over the net (obstacle).

Figure 2-3
Imagine that the net is at least twice as high as it really is.

"In"

A tennis player's second physical priority (with the help of gravity) is to program the ball to land inside of the opponent's court (target).

To gain respect for the net, it is helpful to imagine that it is at least twice as high as it really is (see Figure 2–3). The existence of this "high wall" will force you to become a professional arc maker. These high arcs will usually enable the ball to land deeper in your opponent's court (with a minimum of power).[1] (See Diagram 2–1.)

Deep shots, with high net clearance, accomplish the following:

They greatly reduce the chances of your ball going into the net.

They force your opponent to stand behind the baseline when contacting the ball. It is harder for him to make a winning shot from this position.

They make it more difficult for him to run up to net when he is forced to contact the ball from behind the baseline.

> *Tennis is a game of an obstacle (net) and a target (court). The ball must first clear the obstacle before it can land in the target.*

---

1. The only time you do *not* want your shots to clear the net by a large margin is if your opponent is standing near the net. In such cases, your ball should clear the net by a small margin. Low net clearance will usually cause the net player to contact the ball below the height of the net. When he does so, he will have difficulty producing an offensive shot.

A DRILL TO HELP INCREASE YOUR NET CLEARANCE AND THE DEPTH OF YOUR SHOTS

For this drill, only the large backcourt rectangular box is now considered the target.

Begin rallying with your opponent. Any time a ball does not land in the target, the other player (the one who did not make the mistake) gains the point.

The first player to win 21 points wins.

You will find that the higher the arc of the ball, the easier it is to have the ball land deeply in your opponent's rectangular box. *The depth of a ball should be controlled more through arcs than through power.*

SUMMARY

Tennis is a game that contains two constants: the net and the court.

Tennis is a game that contains two variables: the ball and the strings (racket).

Tennis is a game of a target (court) and an obstacle (net).

A key phrase in tennis is "over and in."

The existence of the net forces the tennis player to become a professional arc maker.

chapter 3

The Senses

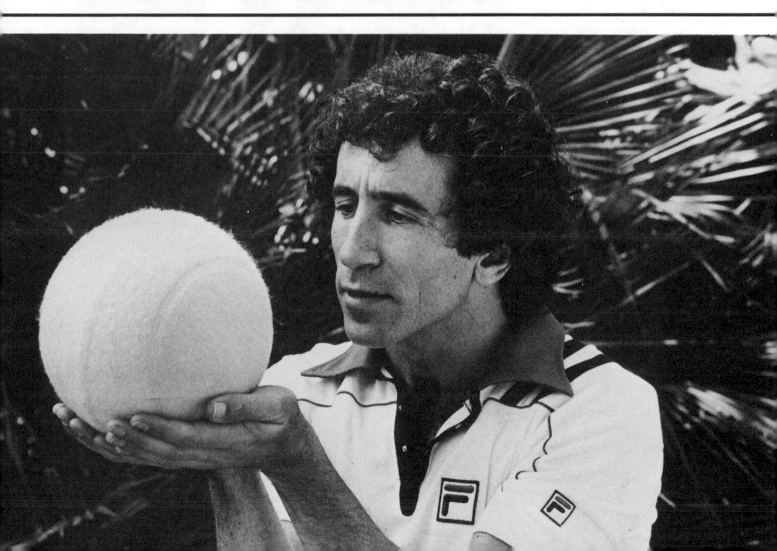

In Chapter 2, we looked at the world outside: the net, the court, the ball, and the racket. Now it's time to look at you, the player. What connects you to the two constants and two variables? The answer is—the senses.

The senses enable you to become a sophisticated tennis computer—calculating the speed of the ball, adjusting the angle of your racket face, determining where to position your body, etc. This chapter will assist you in maximizing your access to that fabulous tennis computer—your senses.

The most important senses to use on a tennis court are sight, touch, and hearing. The purpose of this chapter is to increase your awareness of your senses by supplying you with "sense actions." These actions will improve the chances that precise contact between the ball and strings will be made time after time.

> *The senses are our link between the changing variables and how the body must respond.*

THE SENSE OF SIGHT

The sense of sight supplies us with constantly updated information as to the location of the ball (one of the two variables—see Figure 3–1) and the location of the net and court (two constants). In order to help your eyes do this, imagine that the eyes send out a laser beam that locks onto the ball. When sending out your laser beam the eyes should not be strained or tense. Concentration, not tension, is the connecting force.

Unlike the ball, both the net and court are always stationary. Therefore, your eyes need not focus on these constants with as much intensity or concentration.

Three Critical Focusing Times

Creating the correct relationship (distance) between yourself and the path of the ball is called "lining the ball up." Your sense of sight can be used in a specific fashion in order to help line up the ball. There are three critical focusing times for your eyes. *Try* to focus the eyes on the ball at these three times:

1. As the ball leaves your opponent's strings. Once your opponent contacts the ball, it tends to travel back to you in a straight path. Therefore, watching his moment of contact will give you early information as to where the ball is heading. This information will help you to position yourself in order to properly line up the ball.

2. As the ball lands on your side of the court. Try to see the ball land on your side of the court. This action will also facilitate lining the ball up.

3. As you contact the ball. Try to see the moment of contact between the ball and strings. This will help the precision of the stroke by keeping your head and body still at moment of contact.

Experiment to discover which focusing time is most beneficial to you. You might even find that you like to use all three of them. Eventually you will develop your own system of lining up the ball.

While you are always trying to see and follow the ball, there are two specific times when you will not be very successful.

Figure 3-1
The sense of sight supplies us with constantly updated information as to the location of the ball.

Figure 3-2
The tennis racket allows for an extended reach.

1. Moment of blur. Do not be surprised if you cannot clearly see the moment of contact between the ball and your strings. Only if the ball and strings move toward each other very slowly can you see the contact. At greater speeds, you will see a blur. But it is still important to *try to see the contact*, even if the result is "a moment of blur." Trying to see the contact helps to keep your head stationary at moment of contact. A stationary head at moment of contact increases the chances of a precise tennis stroke.

2. Moment of disappearance. If at moment of contact you are properly keeping your head stationary, after "moment of blur" the ball will probably disappear from your view. Do not panic. It is OK to temporarily lose track of the ball for a fraction of a second. After losing the ball, just raise your head and your eyes will begin tracking it. If you never lose track of the ball, there is an excellent chance that you are raising your head too soon.

An Exercise to Help the Eyes Line the Ball Up

Attach a string to a tennis ball and hang the string from your ceiling. The ball should hang a little lower than your waist. For a minimum of 15 seconds a day, pick up your racket and gently contact the ball. This exercise will make it easier for you to create the correct distance between yourself and the ball once you enter the tennis court.

You can also work on "visual concentration" by just watching the ball (without contacting it) as it swings back and forth.

Figure 3-3
The racket should
feel like an extension
of your right arm—
an enlarged
artificial hand.

(a)

(b)

(c)

If you still have trouble lining the ball up, don't worry. The more hours you play tennis and/or hold the racket, the easier this skill will automatically become.

The Extended Reach

The eyes must line up the ball differently when the player uses a ping-pong paddle, racketball racket, and a tennis racket. The tennis player must learn that because of this long extended reach, he does not have to get too close to the approaching ball. (See Figure 3–2.)

The Direction of the Wind

Your sense of sight also supplies you with information about the prevailing wind.

Awareness of the wind is a valuable skill to develop. Knowing "which way the wind is blowing" will help you to judge what type of shots you should use and to anticipate the speed and direction of your opponent's ball.

As you enter the court, test to see if there is a lot of wind blowing and its direction. A strong wind will affect the direction and distance that the ball travels.

THE SENSE OF TOUCH

We have just discussed how the sense of sight supplies vital information about the ball (the first variable). Similarly, the sense of touch supplies information about the racket (the second variable).

The Right Arm

The racket should *feel* like an extension of your right arm. The strings become an enlarged artificial hand. The reach of your arm has now almost doubled, therefore, the ball must be contacted further away from your body. When you contact the ball with the strings, you should *feel* as though the ball has contacted the middle of your new palm. (See Figures 3–3a through c.)

The Left Hand and Arm

Most people aren't aware that the left hand and arm should be working. In fact, to be a proficient tennis player, you should train your left hand and arm to be almost as dextrous as your racket hand and arm. In this section I am not minimizing the importance of the stronger, racket hand (right); rather, I am emphasizing the importance of a hand that has been neglected.

By touching the throat of the racket as well as the strings, the *left* hand automatically gives information to the brain as to the location of the strings before each stroke begins.

Note: for the left-handed players, naturally everything mentioned about the hands would be reversed.

The Five Finger Pads

The five finger pads (not the tips) of the left hand act as "feeling eyes" (see Figure 3–4). The sense of touch supplies a constant flow of information as to the location of the racket and strings. The index finger pad touches any one (or two) of the strings and the four remaining pads place their imprints gently on the top and bottom of the throat of the racket. The left finger pads touch the racket much the same way a blind person reads in Braille. By using the left hand to touch the strings, you are improving the chances that better contact will consistently be made between the ball and the strings.

Functions of the Left Hand

"Lefty" is "Righty's" younger brother. (See Figures 3–5a and b.) Lefty gets stuck with all the dirty work on the tennis court, yet never gets any of the credit. The following list summarizes Lefty's jobs.

1. Supplies current and accurate information as to the location of the strings.
2. Holds the entire weight of the racket until Righty needs to *take* the racket to produce the stroke.
3. Helps Righty to change grips.
4. Initiates the first backward movement of the racket (backswing) as the stroke begins.

Opposite page: Figure 3-4
The five finger pads.

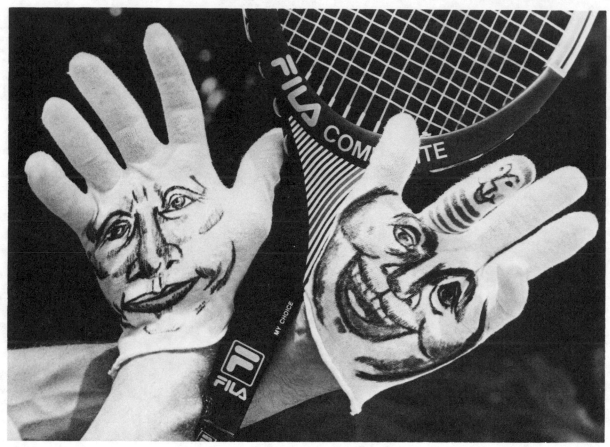

Figure 3-5α
The "Lefty" and "Righty" Brothers.

5. Adjusts the angle of the strings at the beginning of each stroke.

6. Makes minor string corrections depending on the results of the previous stroke.

Lefty should always be free to perform the above jobs. Therefore, during a point the left hand should never be used to hold tennis balls.

The Tennis Racket
Must Become a Part of You

One thing must always occur before you master any sport, craft, art form, or profession. The tool or instrument you use must eventually become a part of you. You will never master anything so long as the object remains a foreign object. The only way to *feel* that the instrument or tool has been assimilated into

your system is to hold the object for long periods of time. That is why music, art, skiing, and tennis teachers always say *practice*. Practicing forces you into holding the object or instrument. It allows the energy that flows through you to eventually flow through your instrument.

Just holding the instrument is the next best thing to practicing. If you can't make it to the court on a daily or weekly basis, try holding a tennis racket every time you talk on the telephone or watch television. You can also practice simulated tennis strokes (slowly) in the privacy of your home or office. This can help to reinforce correct stroke patterns. If a day passes and you haven't touched your racket for at least fifteen seconds, you are probably not a serious tennis player. The tennis racket is a musical instrument that must be touched on a daily basis.

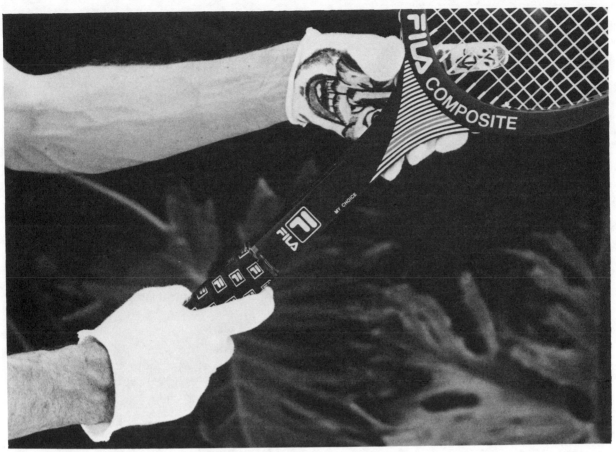

Figure 3-5b
"Lefty" and "Righty" at work.

Touch the Surface of the Court

Touching the surface of the court with your finger pads will reveal a lot of information regarding the speed of the ball after it bounces. The texture of the court determines how fast the ball will travel after it lands. Picture the surface of each court as a huge piece of sandpaper. The coarser the sandpaper, the slower the ball will travel after it bounces. The coarseness creates friction between the court and the ball.

Types of Courts

1. A clay court is like very coarse sandpaper. The speed of the ball after it bounces is relatively slow.
2. A cement court is like medium sandpaper. The speed of the ball after it bounces is medium speed. There is a

huge variation in the coarseness of different cement courts. Some are much faster than others.
3. A grass or wood court is like very fine sandpaper. The speed of the ball after it bounces is very fast on all these surfaces. This is because there is less friction between the ball and surface.

The surface of the court also determines how fast you must prepare your body and the racket before each stroke. The faster the surface the greater your overall state of readiness must be.

THE SENSE OF HEARING
Listen to the Sound of Your Opponent Contacting the Ball

Several years ago in Newport Beach, California, the United States beat South Africa in Davis Cup Competition. In a victorious press conference, Roscoe Tanner was asked about a specific point played. The question was whether the sudden noise from an excited crowd had distracted him. I felt that his answer was quite profound. He said that he hadn't been distracted, but that the noise from the crowd had prevented him from *hearing the sound* of the ball leaving his opponent's strings. Tanner's remarks brought home to me the importance of the sense of hearing in determining the speed and spin of the ball.

When your opponent uses a powerful stroke and a solid and crisp sound results, assume that the ball will be traveling fairly fast. When your opponent uses a powerful stroke but the resulting sound is not solid or crisp, assume the ball will have a lot of spin or that it was mis-hit.

Listen to the Birds

In between points, listen to the sounds around you. This can help you to relax and live in the present, rather than dwelling on a past mistake or worrying about the future.

THE SENSE OF SMELL

For some unknown reason it is difficult to breathe deeply and to worry at the same time. Therefore, become more aware of your breath-ing patterns as well as the smells in the air around you. A few deep breaths or a gentle and rhythmic breathing pattern can help you to relax. Also, avoid holding your breath when the ball and strings meet. Whenever we hold our breath, we are usually worrying about the future or the past.

SUMMARY

To improve your concentration and relaxation, try to perform specific sensory actions during and in between points. While on a tennis court, perform *one* specific sensory action at a time. Do *not* combine sensory actions.

The sense of sight supplies us with moment to moment information as to the location of the ball.

The sense of touch, through the left hand, supplies us with moment to moment information as to the location of the racket and strings.

The sense of hearing supplies us with information as to the speed and spin of the ball.

The sense of smell (breathing) helps us to relax in between and during a point.

chapter
4

Contact

We have already discussed the ball, strings, net, and court and how our senses supply us with information about these variables and constants. Our body must then take this information and use it to make the necessary adjustments that will enable us to properly contact the ball.

The goal of a tennis player is to have the strings accurately and consistently meet the ball. When proper contact occurs, the ball will first fly over the net (obstacle) and will then land in the opponent's court (target area).

The classic tennis stroke has four basic sections: the backswing, the forward motion of the racket, the moment of contact, and the follow-through (referred to in this book as the follow-forward). This chapter focuses on the most important section of the stroke: *contact*. In order to consistently send a ball over the net and into your opponent's court, your body must fully understand this section of the stroke.

CONTACT

The player's entire physical and mental preparation before and during each stroke leads toward the moment of contact. The more experienced the player, the more he understands the importance of this moment.

The *moment of contact* between the ball and strings is the *key to tennis*. It should not be a jarring, abrupt, or fleeting experience. Instead, it is a soothing and tranquil moment in time, a moment that should be *prolonged*. Even if you are running when contact occurs, think of the experience as stillness in motion. The moment of contact must always be treated with respect.

In Chapter 2 we introduced the two main components of the moment of contact—the ball and the racket. But we didn't talk about how they relate to each other during the contact portion of the stroke.

The position of the strings at moment of

Figure 4-1
The strings should be touching on or under, but never above, the equator.

Figure 4-2
The face of the racket.

Figure 4-3a
The up face position.

Figure 4-3b
The down face position.

Figure 4-3c
The flat face position.

contact always determines what part of the ball is touched. This in turn determines the direction in which the ball travels.

> *The Contact Experience is to be prolonged rather than terminated.*

The Equator

Imagine that every ball that approaches you is divided in half by a horizontal ring. This ring is called the *equator* of the ball. (See Figure 4–1.) Regardless of the spin of the ball inside the equator, this horizontal ring is always imagined as being stationary.

At moment of contact, the strings should always be touching *on* or *under the equator* but never above. If the strings touch above the equator, the ball will tend to fly right into the net.[1]

---

1. For tournament level players there may be a few exceptions to this rule.

Position of the Racket Face at Moment of Contact

At moment of contact with the ball, the strings are usually facing in one of three directions. These directions are referred to as the three faces of the racket. (See Figure 4–2.)

1. *Up Face.* At moment of contact with the ball, the face (strings) of the racket is looking *up* at the sky. An up-faced racket touches under the equator of the ball. This produces a ball that flies up in the air. The further under the equator the strings touch, the higher the flight of the ball will tend to be. This up-faced position is also called an open-faced racket (see Figure 4–3a).

2. *Down Face.* At moment of contact with the ball, the face (strings) of the racket is looking down at the ground. A down-faced racket will touch on top of the equator of the ball. This produces a ball that will usually fly into the net. The

Figure 4-4
The direction of the ball (right or left) depends upon which half of the ball (A or B) is contacted.

Figure 4-5a
To direct a ball straight ahead, contact it on the vertical axis.

Figure 4-5b
To direct the ball to the left, contact it "early."

more down-faced the racket, the greater the likelihood of the ball flying into the net. This down-faced position is also called a closed-faced racket (see Figure 4–3b).

3. *Flat Face.* At moment of contact, the face (strings) of the racket is neither up nor down. A flat racket face touches the equator of the ball (see Figure 4–3c). A flat-face racket can successfully produce a solid shot or a topspin shot (see Spin Chapter). (Note also the bent position of the wrist at moment of contact in Figure 4-3c. Placing the wrist in this position will enable you to contact the ball near or a little in front of the front shoe. This wrist position will usually produce the most pleasurable and precise forehands.)

How to Direct the Tennis Ball

We have just talked about how to send the ball up in the air or into the net. Now we're going to discuss how to direct the ball straight ahead, to the left, or to the right.

To understand how to direct a ball, imagine that you have now divided the tennis ball

vertically in half (A and B). The forward direction that the ball travels in is determined by which half is contacted. (See Figure 4–4.)

Directing a Ball Straight Ahead In order to direct the ball straight ahead, the strings should contact the ball on the vertical axis[2]. (See Figure 4–5a.)

Directing a Ball to the Left In order to direct the ball to the left, contact the right side of the ball (see Figure 4–5b). The most practical way to do this is to make contact further in front of the body than you did when you sent the ball straight ahead. This is referred to as "contacting the ball early." If the strings touch the ball too far on the right side of the ball, the ball will respond by flying too far to the left.

Directing a Ball to the Right In order to direct the ball to the right, contact the left side of the ball (see Figure 4–5c). The most

2. While a physicist can find exceptions to this statement by using vector principles, this image can still help you to direct a ball straight ahead.

Figure 4-5c
To direct a ball to the right, contact it "late."

practical way to do this is to make contact a fraction of a second later than you did when you sent the ball straight ahead. This is referred to "as contacting the ball late." If the strings touch the ball too far on the left side of the ball, the ball will respond by flying too far to the right.

Helpful Exercises for Improving the Moment of Contact

Exercise One. Hold the racket with your usual forehand grip but with the palm and strings facing the ceiling (or sky). Place a tennis ball on the strings. Try to slowly roll the ball around the inside edge of the racket without having the ball fall off. Notice that the ball will immediately respond with just a minor movement of the palm.

Exercise Two. With the palm still facing the ceiling (or sky), gently bounce the ball in the middle of the strings. The strings will act like a trampoline. Make sure that the palm rather than the wrist is supplying the energy. This exercise is called *palming up*.

It will help you to learn ball control and how to judge the distance between yourself and the ball.

If you use a two-handed backhand, do this exercise with your left hand. The only difference now is that the left hand is holding the handle farther up the grip (where it usually holds the handle for a two-handed backhand).

Exercise Three. Hold the racket with palm and strings facing the ground. Bounce a ball between the strings and ground without bending or breaking the wrist. Try to have the palm and strings travel gently down while keeping the racket face parallel to the ground. Perform this exercise outside.

The above drills will enable you to:

1. experience how long your new reach is;
2. create the correct distance between yourself and the ball, so that the ball will land *approximately* in the middle of the racket.

3. experience that "racket control" comes from the hand and the arm.

4. feel as if the racket were a part of your body.

Tiny (Four Box) Tennis

Make believe that the four service boxes (the rectangular boxes adjacent to the net) are now the entire boundaries of the tennis court. Any time a ball lands outside a service box it is considered out. Each point is begun with a gentle forehand motion. The ball must always bounce before it is contacted. This game will help you do the following:

It will place more importance on proper contact and less on power.

It will encourage you to shorten your back-swing. This will increase the chances of the strings properly contacting the ball.

It will encourage you to add "touch," "feel," and "control" to your game.

Whether you are a beginner or a tournament player, Tiny Tennis is an excellent way to warm up when you first enter the court. When contacting the ball, make sure that your "gentle control" is coming from a relaxed and loose arm and shoulder. Do not use tension to gain control.

SUMMARY

The moment of contact between the ball and strings is the key to tennis.

The strings of the racket should touch *on* or *underneath* the *equator* of the ball.

chapter 5

The Universal Linear Section of a Stroke

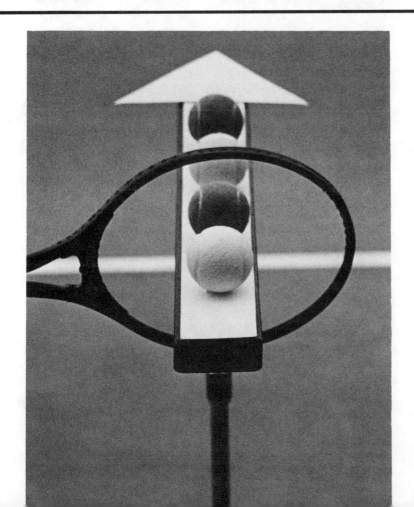

> *Technique is a means to free the artist.*
> *Joseph Chaikin*

Even though most tennis professionals have their own unique form, their strokes have an important common element. I call this element the Universal Linear Section of the stroke. The word universal was chosen because this linear section should appear in all forehand and backhand strokes.

The universal linear section can be described as follows: *During a stroke, regardless of where the racket begins or ends, the strings must travel forward in a straight line, just before, during and just after contact.* This linear section helps to produce a consistently precise stroke. *Regardless of how circular your tennis strokes are, they should also contain a long linear section.*

All pictures, images and stories in this chapter are designed to help you understand what this section is and why it is so important. The pictures in this chapter were designed to encourage you to elongate the universal linear section of the stroke. Therefore, the length of

the linear section (especially for the forehand) may seem exaggerated. Remember that we are talking about the feelings of a linear section and not about the exact length of this section.

PAINT BRUSH RACKET IMAGE

To help you visualize just what the linear section of a stroke is, imagine that your racket has long paint brushes attached to both ends—at the tip of the grip and at the tip of the face. Your goal is to paint two parallel lines on the court just before, during, and after contact. To create these parallel lines (the universal linear section), *the handle and string brushes must travel forward at the same speed.* If the string brush moves forward at a faster speed (ahead of the handle brush), the two parallel lines will no longer be created. To prevent the string brush from moving ahead too soon (a common problem), focus your attention on moving just the handle brush forward. As the handle brush moves forward, the string brush will automatically move forward.

In order to create a linear forehand section, use your palm to supply the energy to move the handle brush forward. (See Figures 5–1a and b.) The arm begins bent and extends (not fully) in order to create the parallel lines.

Figure 5-1
Creating the linear forehand section.

(a)

(b)

(a)   (b)

Figure 5-2
Creating the linear backhand section.

In order to create a linear backhand section, focus more of your attention on your knuckles (or butt of the handle) and less of your attention on the strings. Let the knuckles supply the energy to move the handle brush forward. The arm begins bent and extends in order to create the parallel lines. (See Figures 5–2a and b.)

If you use a two-handed backhand, the *left* palm (for a right-handed player) supplies the energy to move the handle brush forward.

You will notice that the arrows are positioned parallel to the doubles alley. The arrows could also have been placed diagonally across the court. What determines the direction of the arrows is the intended direction of the ball.

GOLF PUTTING IMAGE

Another way to understand the universal linear section is to watch professional golfers as they putt. The golfer either consciously or unconsciously decides what part of the ball he should contact. He then moves the putting iron along a straight line toward that part of the ball.

In Figures 5–3a, b, and c you can see that a channel has been created by two white lines. This linear channel represents the universal

linear section of a stroke. You will notice that before, during, and after contact, the putting iron and strings of the racket both move forward in a linear path through this channel. Just as a circular motion with the putting iron would have jeopardized the putt, so does a circular tennis motion compromise the accuracy and consistency of the tennis stroke. Linear strokes through the channel produce accuracy in both golf and tennis. (Regardless of how circular or powerful your strokes are, they should still pass through a linear channel just before, during, and after contact.)

THE INCORRECT CIRCULAR TENNIS STROKE

The swing (or stroke) that people are most familiar with is the baseball swing, a powerful circular motion. Although this stroke is great for baseball, it should be avoided in tennis. (See Figures 5–4a–c.)

Circular tennis strokes are for gamblers. They resemble a wheel of fortune. Most people realize that the wheel of fortune is a very hard game to win at even once, let alone time after time. Unless your *exact* number comes up, you lose; any number in front of yours or behind yours is worthless. It is an all-or-nothing game, based on pure luck. (See Diagram 5–1.)

With a totally circular tennis stroke it is impossible to predictably *repeat* a stroke because the strings will always tend to be pointing at a different angle each time contact with the ball occurs. Therefore, the strings will tend to touch a different part of the ball each time. This type of non-statistical[1] stroke turns tennis into a game of chance.

1. By non-statistical, I mean that the moment of contact with the ball occurs by chance. A statistical stroke, on the other hand, is a stroke that can be repeated time after time.

Unfortunately, most players have developed this incorrect circular tennis form, where the handle tends to become the center of the wheel and the strings the outside of the wheel. The arm (and racket) follows in an incorrect circular path around the body. The stroke becomes a chancy, non-statistical approach to the sport. (Some circular tennis strokes may even cause tennis elbow.)

During a circular tennis stroke, the strings incorrectly move faster than the handle throughout most of the stroke. This circular motion is usually caused by a very floppy wrist, a tense and continually bent arm, and/or

Figure 5-3
Tennis putting.
(a)

(b)

(c)

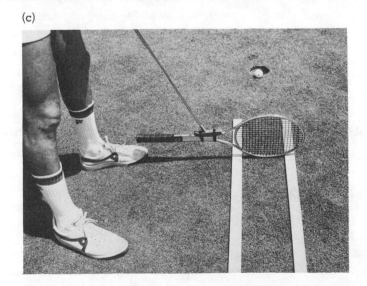

(a)

Figure 5-4
The circular tennis stroke—
avoid it!

(b)

(c)

too much power. You can avoid a circular baseball swing by adding a universal linear section to the middle of each stroke. This will take the "chance" out of your tennis swing.

> *Tennis is a linear sport disguised as a circular sport.*

THE ASCENDING PATH

The universal linear section should also form a gradual *low* to *high* ascending path. This low to high path will encourage the ball to fly over the net. (See Figures 5–5a through d.)

An incorrect high to low path will encourage the ball to fly into the net. This is because the strings will tend to contact the ball above the equator.

RACKETTO AND BALLETTA'S ROMANTIC REUNION

To help you understand and remember the linear concept, let me tell you the parable of Racketto and Balletta's Romantic Reunion.

Ten years had passed since Racketto and Balletta broke their engagement. Racketto had gotten scared at the last minute. Both had searched for ten years to find another mate, but neither was successful. So they both decided to have a wonderfully romantic reunion to see if the once-fiery coals of their love were still hot. They decided to meet on the isolated jungle island of Watuba. There was a small hotel at each end of the long, narrow island, connected by the only road on the entire island. The road was long and straight and had thick jungle vegetation on either side of it. Racketto checked into the North Hotel and Balletta checked into the South Hotel.

When the island church bell sounded on Sunday afternoon, Racketto and Balletta started to walk down the road toward each other. Regardless of how scared each might become, they swore that *neither one would leave the road.* They had no idea of the exact time or exact place of the meeting, but they knew that they would have to meet if neither one left the long straight road. They came closer and closer. Finally, by a large palm tree, they had their long awaited reunion. They made gentle, caressing, tender, and loving contact with one another. (Ah, youth.)

Contact occurred because both had continued directly down the same path toward one another. Neither one had left the road for even a second. Neither one had known where or when they would meet, but both had the perseverance that led to their wonderful contact.

Just in case you don't care for romantic parables, let's spell out what happened. Balletta, of course, is the tennis ball and Racketto is the racket. The long road is the path of the approaching tennis ball. Notice in Diagram 5–2 that Racketto could have met Balletta at points 11, 10, 9, 8, 7, 6, or 5. Any one of these meeting places would have produced a successful reunion, as long as both had stayed on the linear path.

Balletta and Racketto's potential meeting places (contact areas 11 to 5) can also be called *multiple contact options.* These numerous opportunities for meeting the ball are only possible with a linear stroke. If, however, Racketto's strings had gone ahead of his handle, he would have produced a circular stroke with only a single contact possibility. Obviously, it is preferable to have a stroke that presents more than one opportunity to contact the ball.

TIMING

If you were an athletic genius who practiced many hours a day, you would probably have near-perfect timing. You would rarely miss a shot. If you were such a player, you could get away with a fairly circular tennis stroke. John McEnroe, Martina Navratilova, and Ilie Nastase are three such players.

Diagram 5-1
The wheel of fortune's incorrect circular motion.

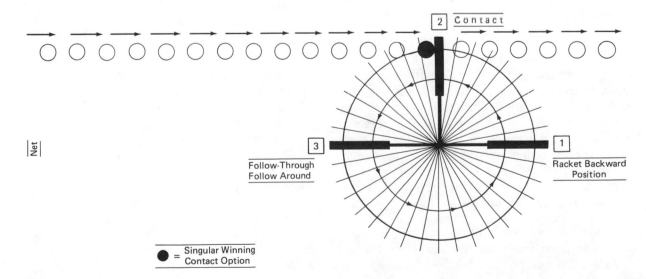

Net

3 Follow-Through Follow Around

2 Contact

1 Racket Backward Position

● = Singular Winning Contact Option

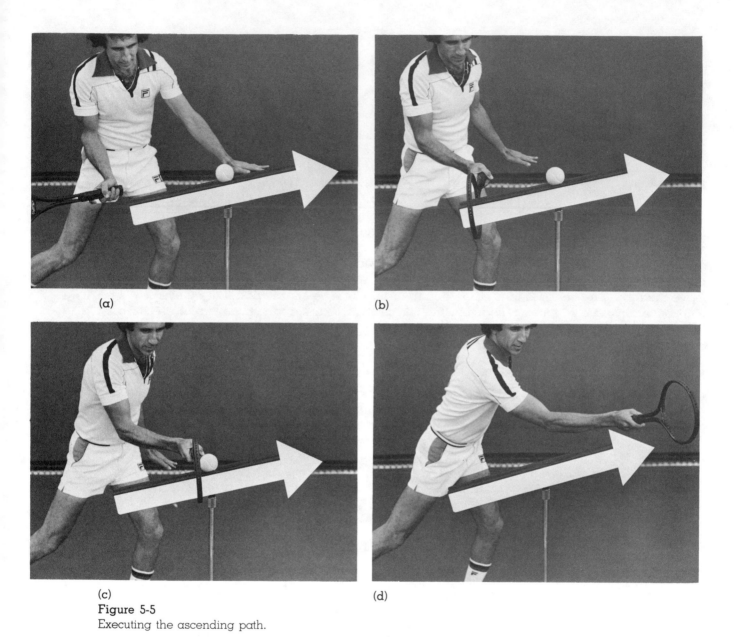

(a)

(b)

(c)

(d)

Figure 5-5
Executing the ascending path.

If, however, you are not an athletic genius, your timing on the court will almost always be a little off, making it virtually impossible to create a consistent, statistical stroke using a totally circular stroke. Because you will never know exactly where or when contact will occur, a universal linear section is needed within each stroke to create multiple contact options. The more gifted a player's timing, the shorter the linear contact section will need to be.

Regardless of how gifted you are, create a long linear contact section within each stroke. This section will provide a safety back-up sys-

tem that will guarantee better percentage tennis strokes. The backhand strokes of Jimmy Connors, Chris Evert Lloyd, Ivan Lendl, Tracy Austin, and Vitas Gerulaitis are wonderful visual examples of linear form.

By creating a stroke that contains a universal linear section, you can make contact anywhere along the linear section (multiple contact options) and the accuracy of your shot will not be jeopardized (see Figures 5–6a and b.).

The pictures in the Forehand and Backhand chapters are all designed to help you produce a pleasurable universal linear contact section.

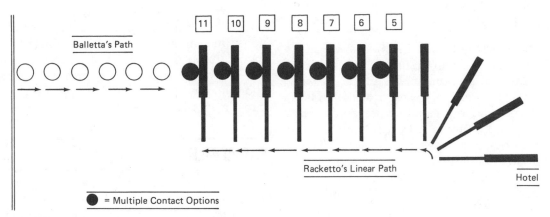

Diagram 5-2
Multiple contact options.

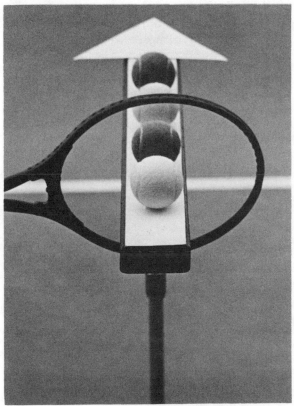

(a)
Figure 5-6
Creating a stroke with a universal linear section.

(b)

HOW A STROKE WITH A LINEAR SECTION SHOULD FEEL

Your body is *not* naturally inclined to want to produce a stroke with a linear section (especially on the forehand side). In fact, it will probably reject this concept for a while. Therefore, you must have patience when first learning to produce a stroke with a linear section.

Remember that when producing a linear section, the body should experience pleasurable sensations. The linear section should *not* be created by using a restrictive, tension-filled or painful motion. Rather, the shoulder and arm should remain free, loose and relaxed. The shoulder and arm should *never* punch, push, poke, or jab at the ball to create this section. The shoulder and arm should also never be locked, stiff, or straight.

A stroke with a linear section should also be completed naturally with pleasurable fluidity. It should never be prematurely stopped. It should feel like an enjoyable, expressive, and elongated ballet motion. Note: On the forehand side, the momentum of the racket will naturally create a partially circular follow-through motion. This slight curve is acceptable when it comes *after* a long linear contact section.

If you have tried for *many* hours to experience pleasurable strokes with long linear sections, and are still unsuccessful, then and only then shorten the length of the linear section. Use this as a last resort, however, because short linear sections tend to produce totally circular tennis strokes.

SUMMARY

Just before, during, and just after contact, the strings must travel in a straight line, regardless of your tennis form. This part of the stroke is referred to as the universal linear section.

Each linear stroke has multiple contact options, providing many opportunities to properly contact the ball.

The universal linear section should form a gradual low to high ascending path. This low to high path will encourage the ball to fly over the net.

Unless you have perfect timing, you should never use a completely circular stroke.

chapter
6

The Forehand

Regardless of how primitive or advanced your tennis game is, you undoubtedly have some kind of forehand and backhand stroke. The motion you use when trying to contact the ball on the right side (regardless of what the motion looks like) is your forehand, and the motion you use when trying to contact the ball on the left side is your backhand. (Remember, if you are left-handed, the sides are reversed.)

Other than telling you on what side your body contacts the ball, these names are just labels. In fact, for learning purposes, it might be helpful if I changed the names of the forehand, backhand, serve, and volley to kabba, sabba, gabba, and fabba respectively. This way you wouldn't have any preconceived ideas of what each stroke should be. When I talked about the sabba, you could listen with a totally open mind. You wouldn't bring any prejudices or fears with you.

When learning or improving a specific tennis stroke, you will find it most helpful to think of the motion as being composed of a series of actions. Then, by just adding a few simple actions to your current motion, you can improve your strokes dramatically. This "specific action approach" is just as valid for the beginner as it is for the advanced player.

Both the Forehand and Backhand chapters begin by dealing with these simple yet effective actions. Then the entire strokes are discussed from beginning to end. Both chapters have been organized similarly, as follows:

1. The most important parts of the body used in producing a tennis stroke.
2. Directing a forehand.
3. Simple actions to apply to your current strokes.
4. An in-depth look at each part of a full tennis stroke.
5. Tennis imagery actions that will help you to perform the most important actions of the stroke.
6. A summary.

THE MOST IMPORTANT PARTS OF THE BODY USED IN PRODUCING A FOREHAND STROKE

While many parts of the body come into play to produce a forehand stroke, the most important are the hand, wrist, arm, and shoulder. These are closest to the racket and are therefore most important in controlling the racket and its path.

Figure 6-1
The "ball joint" or "palm index knuckle."

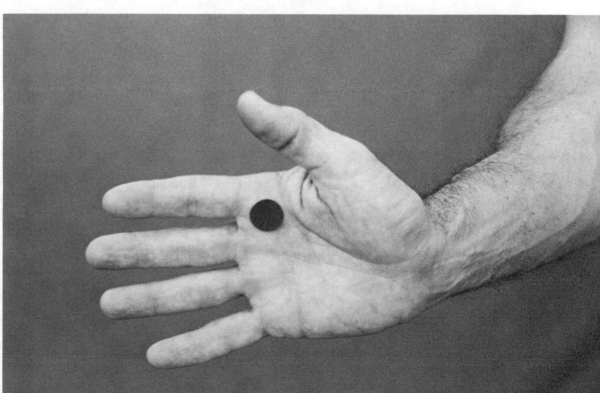

The more parts of the body that move during a stroke, the harder it is to produce an accurate and consistent stroke. Excessive use of the legs and hips tends to hinder the accuracy and consistency of a stroke, and should therefore be left to the very advanced player. With the exception of the hand and arm, you should try to take most of the body motion out of a forehand stroke. I learned just how important the arm is in producing a tennis stroke while teaching wheelchair tennis at Widney High School in Los Angeles. By just moving their arms, most students were able to produce a variety of strokes, even though they were sitting in wheelchairs.

Even though we will be looking at each of these four parts of the body separately, it is really impossible to disassociate one part from another. For example, when we discuss the motion of the hand, this does not mean that the arm is not functioning. You must keep in mind that the palm of the hand, wrist, arm, and shoulder are of course all connected and interrelated.

The Palm

The importance of the *palm* in the forehand stroke cannot be overemphasized. The hand is the focal point for four vital functions.

Directing the Ball. The hand is the only part of the body that touches the racket at moment of contact. The palm guides the racket, which in turn directs the ball. *The palm should be traveling forward toward your intended target just before, during, and just after the strings contact the ball.* The palm helps to create the linear section of the forehand. (A more detailed explanation of directing the ball appears later in this chapter.)

Your strokes can become even more precise by selecting a *specific area* of your palm as the guidance system. A portion of the palm that is very helpful in directing the ball is the joint at the base of the index finger—the "ball joint" (i.e., the "palm index knuckle") (see Figure 6–1). Experiment to determine what portion of your palm is most helpful in directing the ball.

Feeling the Ball. Even though the strings are contacting the ball, the vibration that you receive should feel as though the palm is actually contacting the ball. The palm should be the focal feeling point of each stroke. The forehand can be thought of as a *palmular stroke* (see Figure 6–2).

Energizing the Ball. The palm should also be thought of as the *energy source*. Most players

Figure 6-2
Think of the forehand as a palmular stroke.

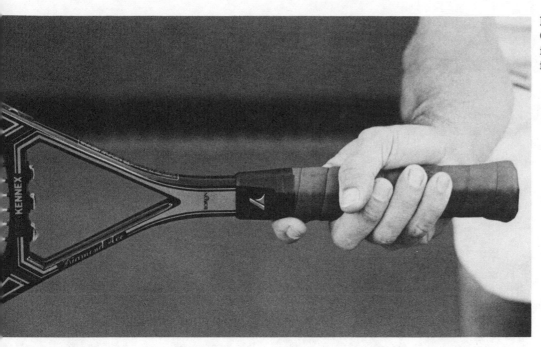

incorrectly think of the strings as the energy source. When this occurs, a chancy, "wristy" circular stroke will usually be created. When the palm becomes the energy source, however, a stroke that contains an elongated linear section will be created. *The palm initiates the forward momentum of the racket*; the strings do not. Think *"palm power"* rather than "wrist or string power."

Creating the Grip. The easiest and most versatile forehand grip is called the Eastern Forehand Grip. Before learning a more advanced grip (the Western Forehand Grip), be sure you know how to use and are comfortable with the Eastern Forehand Grip. The hardest and least versatile forehand grip is called the Continental Forehand Grip. Try not to use this grip unless you are serving or playing the net. (Refer to Chapter 13 for pictures and details.)

The Wrist

Each forehand should contain minimal wrist movement. By minimizing the use of the wrist, a linear section can be produced as the racket travels in a straight line before, during, and after contact with the ball. If you have excessive wrist movement, the racket is more likely to create an inconsistent circular stroke. Circular strokes are produced by incorrectly moving the wrist to slap or swat at the ball. A firm

yet receptive[1] wrist will create minimal wrist movement.

To create a firm yet receptive wrist, do one or all of the following:

Move the hand at least an additional inch up the handle. This will promote the use of the palm and improve the accuracy of your forehand by diminishing the incorrect use of an excessive wrist motion. Whenever you are mis-hitting the forehand, experiment by moving your hand up the handle a little. This upward movement of the palm is called choking up (see Figure 6–3). By moving your hand in the opposite direction (down the handle) you can increase the power and fluidity of the stroke, although the precision of your shot will usually be jeopardized.

Create a space between the index and middle finger. This space helps to create a "palmular sensation" at moment of contact. Extending the index finger makes the racket feel lighter and automatically firms up the wrist.

1. By "receptive" I mean that the wrist will be able to feel and receive the vibration between the ball and the strings at moment of contact. It will not be rigid, locked, brittle, or tense. Note that in extreme emergencies—for example, the ball has passed you by—wrist action will be necessary.

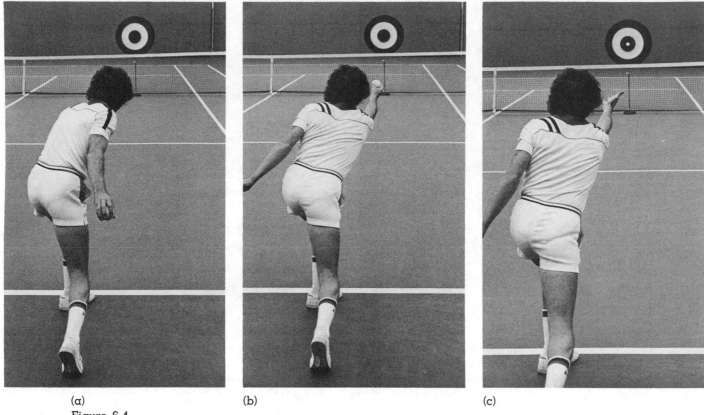

(a)   (b)   (c)

Figure 6-4
A pleasurable and fluid tennis stroke is like a throwing or bowling motion.

Gently squeeze the bottom three fingers (pinky, ring, and middle) of your grip hand just before and during contact with the ball. This will create a firm yet receptive wrist. After completing the stroke, relax your hand until you're ready to make contact once again.

The Arm

The forehand stroke should be a pleasurable experience, with the arm free of tension and strain. As it produces the stroke, the arm should feel long, loose, and relaxed. While creating the stroke, the arm should never push, jab or poke at the ball. At the completion of the stroke, the arm should never be locked, rigid, or tense. (See the Stroke Fluidity Section in Chapter 1.)

The Shoulder While the arm is producing the forehand motion, the shoulder should always be in a loose and natural state. At moment of

contact, the shoulder should never be tensed or raised up toward the ear. Do *not* try to control your shots by tensing the shoulder or neck.

Before, during, and after contact, the shoulder should *not* have any idea of where the ball is going. At moment of contact, the shoulder should be in a pleasurable and ignorant state. Only the palm of the right hand should have "directional control" information.

The Elbow Try not to focus your attention on the elbow when producing the forehand ground stroke. Focusing your attention on the elbow tends to produce a tense and pushy forehand. Focus on the palm and shoulder instead.

DIRECTING A FOREHAND

Now that we have discussed the palm, arm, and shoulder, let's see how they can be applied to the pleasure and precision of your forehand.

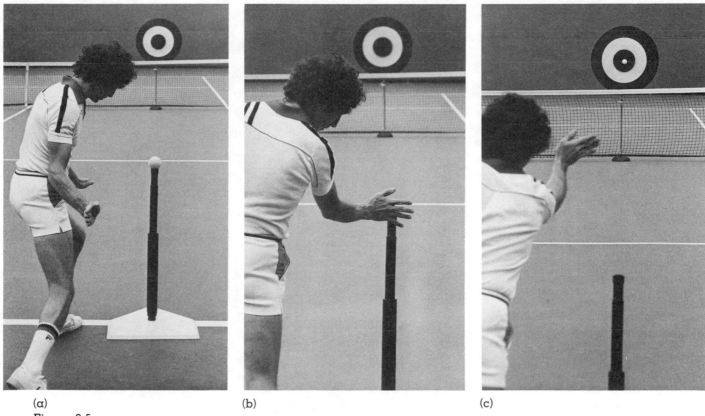

(a)   **(b)**   **(c)**

Figure 6-5
The palm should travel in a forward path to the target (a) before, (b) during, and (c) after contact.

The Pleasure of a Forehand

When producing a forehand, you should receive pleasure in the arm and shoulder. To simulate this experience, place a ball in the hand that usually holds the handle of the racket. Stand with your side to the net, and throw the ball underhand. This relaxed throwing (or bowling) motion is very similar to a pleasurable and fluid tennis stroke (see Figures 6–4a through c).

The Precision of a Forehand

If you were forced to contact the ball with your palm (as in handball), rather than your racket, you would immediately realize that the palm is the directional focal point of a forehand. Your palm would automatically travel in a forward path toward your intended target before, during, and after contact (see Figures 6–5a through c). You would immediately realize that

the precision of your stroke would be compromised if your palm created an excessively circular non-linear motion.

Combining the Pleasure and Precision Principles

Now you are ready to create the forehand stroke with your racket. Because your strings are just an extension of your palm, your strings now need to do the same thing that was just done by your palm. The strings should therefore travel in a forward path toward your intended target before, during, and after contact. (See Figures 6–6a through c.)

Although you are actually hitting the ball, the *feeling* should be one of throwing your palm toward your intended target. It should feel as though the *palm* leaves the body, flies over the net, and lands in the target area. (See Figure 6–6d.) Imagine that, at moment of contact, your palm becomes a tennis ball. Never

(a)

(b)

(c)

Figure 6-6
The strings should travel in a forward path to the target (a) before, (b) during, and (c) after contact.

try "to hit" the ball to the target. "Hitting" will create a tense and circular stroke. Rather, throw your palm to the target.

To receive additional fluidity, you can imagine that the right shoulder also flies over the net and lands in your intended area.

SIMPLE ACTIONS TO APPLY TO YOUR CURRENT STROKE

The following section contains simple yet effective *actions* that can immediately be applied to your current forehand stroke.

These same actions are also important elements of the entire full stroke motion that will be introduced in the next section.

Hold the Racket with the Left Finger Pads—"Lefty"

As you are waiting for the ball to be returned, have the left finger pads hold the weight of the racket. This will enable the right hand, arm,

and shoulder to remain relaxed and free of tension. The left index finger should touch the strings. Knowing where the strings are before the stroke begins will increase the chances that proper contact will occur between the ball and the strings. (Refer back to the Senses Chapter.)

Bring the Racket Back as Soon as Possible

Bring the racket back *before* the ball bounces on your side. Even when you don't take a full backswing, or when you are running a short distance for the ball, complete the entire backswing *before* the ball bounces on your side. Early preparation of the racket will enable you to be prepared to return both slow and very fast moving balls. (See Figure 6–7.)

Prolong the Moment of Contact

Try to prolong the moment of contact between the racket and the ball by using a fluid, pleasurable motion. This will enable you to:

(d)
Imagine you are throwing your palm toward your intended target.

1. Create a stroke with minimal wrist movement.
2. Create a linear section before, during and after contact.
3. Produce more of a linear and less of a circular follow-through motion.

AN IN-DEPTH LOOK AT EACH PART OF A FULL FOREHAND STROKE

The following pages contain a detailed breakdown of a simulated forehand tennis stroke. The stroke is broken down into six sections. (The backhand stroke also contains the same six sections.)

FH 1: Racket Ready Alert Position
FH 2: Racket Backward
FH 3: Stepping Forward Section
FH 4: Racket Forward Section

FH 5: Linear Contact Section
FH 6: Follow-Forward (Follow-Through) Section

The best place to explore each section of the forehand is off the tennis court, where you won't have to worry about a ball coming toward you. If you do practice these sections on the court, make sure that the ball is approaching at a very slow speed. When producing the stroke, create a gentle, soft, and soothing motion.

Note: Some people love it when a stroke is broken down into its component parts. Others, however, get psyched-out. If it is going to make you nervous to look at an in-depth breakdown of the forehand stroke, then just glance at the pictures in this section and go directly to the next part of this chapter—Additional Imagery Actions, page 61.

FH 1:
Ready Alert Position

Much of the time you spend on the court is taken up with waiting and/or preparing for the return of the ball. This important and valuable time should not be wasted. Just before your opponent contacts the ball, your racket and body should be in the Ready Alert Position. (See Figure 6–8.)

The following functions should be performed while in this position.

1. The racket is out in front of the body and acts as a line that divides the body in half.
2. The left hand ("Lefty") holds almost the entire weight of the racket.
3. The left finger pads receive information about the exact location of the strings and racket and send the information to the brain.
4. The left hand is also waiting to help the right hand to make any grip changes that might be necessary.
5. The right hand, arm, and shoulder are totally loose and natural.
6. The legs are spread apart and slightly bent. Most of the bending is done from the knees rather than the waist.

Figure 6-7
Bring the racket back before the ball bounces on your side.

7. The weight is equally distributed on the balls of the feet (heels are *not* touching the ground).

FH 2:
Beginning of
the Racket Backward Section

At the very beginning of the racket backward section, the left hand adjusts the angle of the strings (up face, flat face, down face) according to the results of the previous stroke. Example: If the last forehand stroke barely cleared the net, the left hand should further open up the face of the racket (an infinitesimal adjustment) for the next stroke. (See Figures 6–9a through c.)

The left hand should let go *immediately* after adjusting the angle of the strings.

Completion of
the Racket Backward Section

Many players believe that the same amount of backswing is appropriate to all occasions. This is a misconception. The main purpose of bringing the racket back is to give additional power to the ball. If the ball approaching you is moving slowly, a bigger backswing is needed. If, however, the ball approaching already has sufficient power (speed), a big backswing isn't as necessary. *Bringing the racket back is a variable, not a constant.* (See Figure 6–10.)

As soon as your eyes determine that the ball is coming to the forehand side, prepare

Figure 6-8
The ready alert position.

(a)

(b)

Figure 6-9

At the beginning of the racket backward section,
the left hand slightly adjusts the strings in one of
three directions.

(c)

Figure 6-10
Completion of the racket backward section.

Figure 6-11
Stepping forward.

Figure 6-12
The racket forward section.

the racket by bringing it back to the appropriate position. Preparing the racket early is vital to a successful tennis stroke. Complete the backswing (regardless of its size) *before* the ball bounces on your side of the court. The only time you might have to abandon this early racket preparation is if you are forced to run full speed to get to a ball. (This early racket preparation will also not apply if you use a continuous-motion high-loop backswing.)

As the racket is brought back, most of the weight is transferred onto the right foot. If time permits, you can also take a series of small steps that will enable the left hip to turn and directly face the net (picture not shown). At the completion of this turn most of the weight would still be on the right foot.

FH 3: Stepping Forward

To help maintain your balance and encourage the fluidity of the stroke, transfer your weight forward to your left foot. (See Figure 6–11.)

FH 4: Racket Forward Section

During this section, the racket is brought forward toward the approaching ball. Most of the power of a stroke comes from this section. (See Figure 6–12.)

FH 5: Linear Contact Section

Contact should occur somewhere within the linear contact section. The longer the linear section, the more multiple contact options, and the greater the likelihood of producing a consistent and precise tennis stroke. (See Figures 6–13a through c.)

During the linear contact section, the arm begins bent and extends forward.[2] The handle and strings travel straight toward the intended target with neither the handle nor the strings going ahead of the other. This "tie" between the handle and strings can be accomplished by exaggerating the *feeling* that the palm, not the strings, is the energy source.

Because the ball must clear the net, the palm and racket should complete the stroke higher than the net. This is accomplished by having the palm and racket traveling in a gradual low to high linear path.

While it is physically impossible to carry the ball on the strings for an extended period of time, the *feeling* during this section should be one of *prolonged contact between the ball and the strings.*

FH 6: Follow-Forward (Linear Follow-Through) Section

The linear section of the stroke leads directly into the follow-forward—the final section of the forehand.

In traditional instruction, the motion that completes the stroke has been called the follow-through. As previously mentioned, however, this typical forehand follow-through usually contains an excessively circular motion that can jeopardize or even eliminate the entire linear contact section. Therefore, to avoid the pitfalls of an excessively circular follow-through, think of this section as the follow-*forward*. Rather than circular fluidity, create linear fluidity. (See Figure 6–14.)

The easiest way to develop a follow-forward motion is to maintain a relatively unchanging wrist position throughout the *entire* stroke. This can be accomplished by having the *feeling* that the palm flows forward toward the net for an extended period of time. The follow-forward motion can also be created by *prolonging* the "carrying" sensation during the linear section.

Note: For anatomical reasons, the forehand is naturally a more circular motion than the backhand. It is therefore very easy to produce a circular follow-through motion on the forehand. There is nothing intrinsically wrong with circular follow-throughs as long as they come *after a long linear section.* The problem with most people's forehands, however, is that their circular follow-throughs either minimize or eliminate the entire linear contact section. When this occurs, the precision and consistency of the stroke are jeopardized. (For this reason I have intentionally omitted a picture of a circular follow-through.)

After completing a stroke, you may notice that your strings are farther ahead of the handle than Figure 6–14 would indicate, resulting in a slightly circular motion. Note, however, that this partially circular path has been cre-

---

2. Though the arm extends it never becomes fully extended, straight, or locked.

(a)

Figure 6-13
The linear contact
section.

(b)

(c)

ated by the natural momentum of the coasting racket, rather than any intentionally circular motion that you might have generated. (The *ideal* length of the racket's circular path should be approximately one-eighth of a full circle. The *maximum* length of the racket's circular path should be a quarter of a full circle.) Remember, your job is just to produce a graceful and fluid linear follow-forward motion, even though the strings (on their own) might be creating a partially circular motion.

> *Maximize the linear section and minimize the circular follow-through.*

ADDITIONAL IMAGERY ACTIONS

The following images will help you to improve the linear and follow-forward sections of a stroke.

The Tube Image To help create a linear section (on both forehand and backhand), picture that your racket is traveling through a long, straight, cylindrical tube. As the racket is traveling through this imaginary tube, it should feel as though the *strings* are *carrying* the ball forward. This linear tubular image will help you to maximize the use of the palm and to minimize the use of the wrist (See Figures 6–15a through d.)

To perform this tubular motion, do the following:

Have the palm initiate the forward movement of the racket. This can be done by "throwing" the palm forward and over the net.

Contact the ball *on* or a little *below the equator.* (Contacting the ball above the equator usually results in a ball going into the net.)

Given the height of the net, imagine that the tube is pointed slightly up, like a cannon, so that the palm and strings travel low to high. This low to high motion will encourage the ball to fly over the net.

The arm should extend naturally in a graceful, gentle, and fluid motion.

If your forehand contains a circular follow-through, make sure it occurs *after* the strings have traveled through the *entire* length of the tube.

Candy Cane Image The path of the racket should create a candy cane as it flows forward. This image will help you to elongate the linear and follow-forward sections of a stroke. A linear follow-forward feeling will help to guarantee the production of a long linear contact section. (See Figures 6–16a through d.)

When producing the candy cane remember the following:

Figure 6-14
The follow-forward
(linear follow-through) section.

(a)

(b)

(c)

(d)

Figure 6-15
Picture your racket as traveling through a long, straight, cylindrical tube.

Get the feeling that the strings are "carrying" the ball throughout the entire straight section of the cane.

The more power you add to your stroke, the *longer* your candy cane should be.

Let the palm of the right hand initiate the forward momentum of the racket.

Let the shoulder and arm *naturally* complete the follow-forward motion. Never prematurely stop the natural forward flow of

the racket. Any circular motion should occur after Figure 6–16d.

Tell Your Target "Happy Birthday" Decide where you want your ball to land. This is your target area. Pretend there is an invisible opponent standing in your target area and that today is his/her birthday. Next, make believe that you have attached a birthday card to the face of your racket. Throughout the linear contact section tell your target and invisible opponent

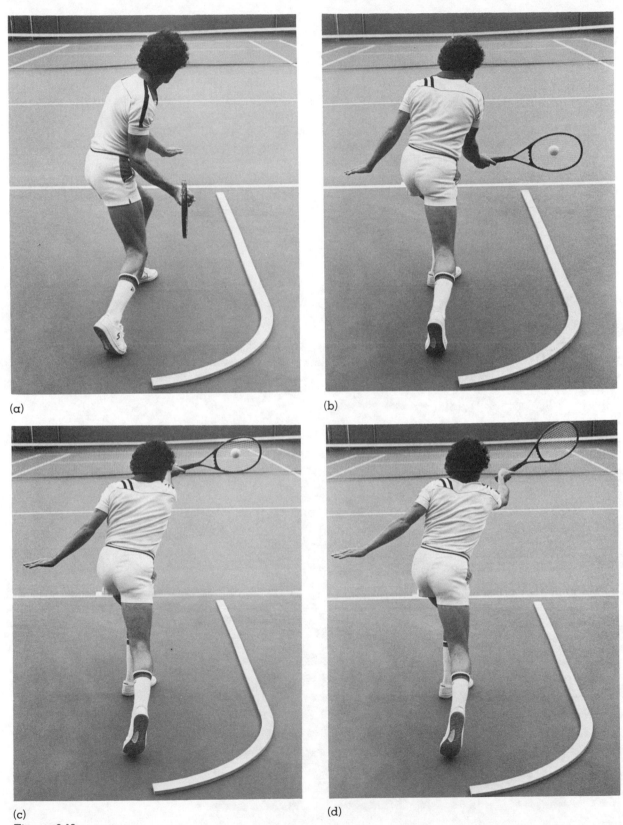

(a)

(b)

(c)

(d)

Figure 6-16
The path of the racket should create a candy cane as it flows forward.

"Happy Birthday." (See Figure 6–17.) This image will encourage you to elongate the linear contact section.

A HIGH FOREHAND STROKE

There are times when you will be forced to contact the ball above your head. When this occurs, it is considered a high forehand stroke. This stroke should be thought of as a defensive or neutralizing stroke, rather than as an offensive stroke. For this reason, your shot should fly in a high arc over the net and land fairly deeply in your opponent's court.

The high forehand stroke is illustrated by the horse race image in Figures 6–18. Handle horse and string horse race along two high parallel horizontal lines. *Handle* horse is *always winning* the race from beginning to end. This motion will enable the strings to touch on or *under* the equator of the ball during the entire stroke. (See Figures 6–18a through 6–18e.) It is easier to produce this stroke when your side is to the net, and your weight has been transferred onto the front foot. The arm

Figure 6-17
Throughout the linear contact section, tell your target "Happy Birthday."

(a)

(b)

Figure 6-18
Handle horse should always
be winning the race,
from beginning to end.

(c)

(d)

(e)

and racket should produce a flowing and gliding forward motion rather than a pushing or punching motion. Make sure your *palm remains high* in the air throughout this entire linear stroke.

Notice that the *left* hand (not right) lifts the racket up to the height of the oncoming ball.

SUMMARY

The forehand should be a pleasurable physical experience. The arm and shoulder should be free of tension and strain throughout the *entire* stroke.

The racket should be brought back as soon as possible. It should never be brought back more than is necessary.

The right palm directs, feels, and energizes the ball.

Rather than hitting the ball, imagine that you are throwing your palm over the net and into your intended target.

Rather than hitting the ball, imagine that the racket is carrying the ball over the net.

The linear contact section should be elongated.

A linear follow-forward motion should be created rather than an excessive circular follow-through motion.

The forehand should contain more linear fluidity and less circular fluidity.

At the completion of the forehand, the palm and strings should be at a height higher than the net.

chapter 7

The Backhand

The purpose of this chapter is to demystify the backhand. As you follow the actions and imagery presented in the following pages, you'll find that the pleasure, precision, and consistency of your backhand will increase significantly.

The main similiarity between the forehand and backhand is that both strokes contain an elongated linear section. The main difference between the strokes is that the racket's follow-forward path is more circular on the forehand and more linear on the backhand.

Anatomically, the backhand stroke is easier than the forehand, because it is more natural for the arm to produce a linear path on the backhand side than on the forehand side. Yet the majority of players have backhands that are much weaker than their forehands. In fact just the word backhand is enough to send chills down the spine of many players.

There are a number of reasons for this.

Habit: In baseball and golf, a right-handed player always lines the ball up on the right side of the body. If a tennis player ever plays these other sports, he is initially more comfortable lining the ball up on the right side of his body (forehand) than on the left side (backhand). On the backhand side, footwork and body preparation will therefore initially feel less comfortable.

Balance: When a player is off balance, he has more difficulty creating a linear section.

Grip: Many players use the wrong backhand grip. Their hand and wrist are therefore in a weak and uncomfortable position at moment of contact. An incorrect grip can prevent a player from ever developing a sophisticated backhand stroke. (See Grip chapter.) The most versatile one-handed grip is called the Eastern Backhand Grip. Before learning another grip (Continental Backhand Grip) be sure you are comfortable with and know how to use the Eastern Backhand Grip. (Refer to the Grip chapter for pictures and details.)

Circular vs. Linear: Most players incorrectly create circular backhands, thus jeopardizing their chances of contacting the ball.

Basically there are two types of backhand strokes—the one-handed backhand and the two-handed backhand. Despite the fact that the two-handed backhand is easier for many

Figure 7-1
The pinky knuckle is the focal point of the backhand.

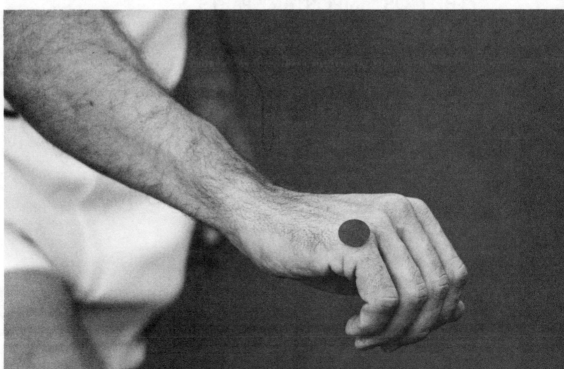

Figure 7-2
You should feel as though
the pinky knuckle,
or butt of the handle,
were contacting the ball.

people, the one-handed backhand seems to be used more frequently. For this reason it will be discussed first and in more depth.

THE MOST IMPORTANT PARTS OF THE BODY THAT PRODUCE A BACKHAND STROKE

The backhand stroke is primarily an arm motion. As with the forehand, excessive use of the legs and hips only hinders the potential accuracy of the stroke.

The Knuckles

For the one-handed backhand stroke the importance of the *knuckles* cannot be overemphasized. The knuckles (especially the pinky knuckle) are the focal point for three vital functions:

1. *Directing the ball:* The hand is the only part of the body that touches the racket at moment of contact. Therefore, it is the knuckles that guide the racket, which in turn directs the ball. The most important knuckle to focus your attention on is the pinky knuckle. (See Figure 7–1.) The pinky knuckle should be traveling forward toward your intended target just before, during, and after the strings contact the ball. This will help create a linear contact section. (A more detailed explanation of directing the ball appears later in this chapter.)

2. *Feeling the ball:* Even though the strings are contacting the ball, the vibration that you receive should *feel* as though the pinky knuckle (or the butt of the handle) were actually contacting the ball. (See Figure 7–2.)

3. *Energizing the ball:* The pinky knuckle should always be thought of as the *energy source.* Most players mistake the

Opposite page: Figure 7-3
Throughout the backhand, it should feel as if knuckle number one were leading knuckle number four.

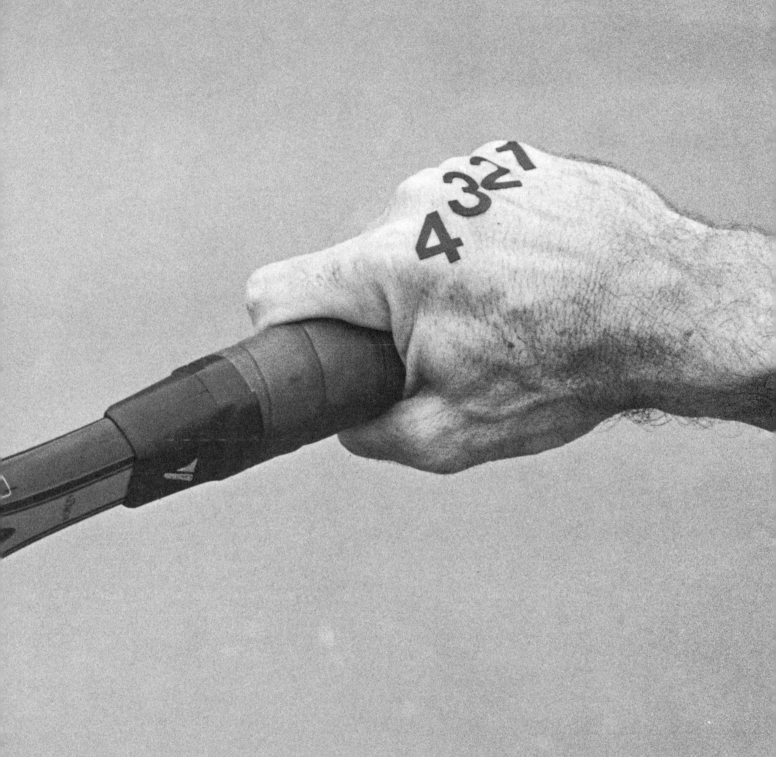

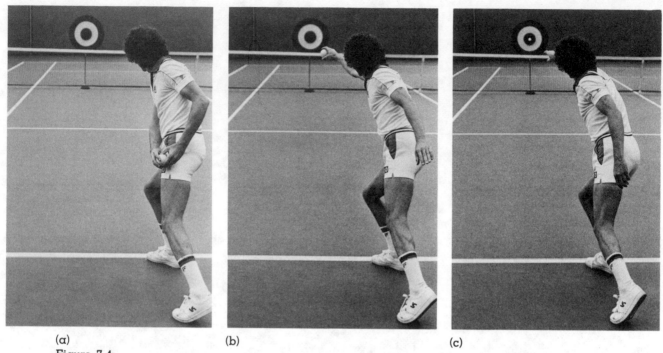

(a)   (b)   (c)

Figure 7-4
With your right side to the net, throw the ball underhand with the knuckles facing the net.

strings for the energy source. When this occurs, a chancy, "wristy" circular stroke will usually be created. When the pinky knuckle becomes the energy source, however, a stroke that contains an elongated linear section will be created. *The pinky knuckle initiates the forward momentum of the racket*, the strings do not. Think "*pinky knuckle power*" rather than "wrist or string power."

The main reason for focusing your attention on the pinky knuckle is to prevent the index knuckle from moving ahead of the other knuckles (see Figure 7–3). If the index knuckle (4) goes ahead of the pinky knuckle (1), the strings will produce a "chancy" circular motion. Therefore, whenever the racket is moving forward (including the completion), it should *feel* as though the pinky knuckle is leading the index knuckle. This action will help the strings to produce a long linear section. The pinky knuckle (or butt of the handle) should always *feel* as though it is ahead of the index knuckle or tied with the index knuckle, but never behind it.

If you have difficulty focusing your attention on just the pinky knuckle, don't worry. Shift your attention to all of the knuckles (excluding the thumb knuckle) and have all the knuckles direct, feel, and energize the ball. During the entire linear contact section all of the knuckles should travel forward toward your intended target. The knuckles are now tied in a "photo finish" as they move forward producing the linear contact section. Once again, make sure that the index knuckle does not go ahead of the pinky knuckle. If it does, the strings will incorrectly produce a circular motion.

The Wrist

To become more consistent, *eliminate all wrist movement* from your backhand. Without any wrist movement a linear contact section and linear follow-forward section can be produced as the racket travels in a straight line before, during, and after contact with the ball. If you use excessive wrist movement, the racket is more likely to create an inconsistent circular stroke.

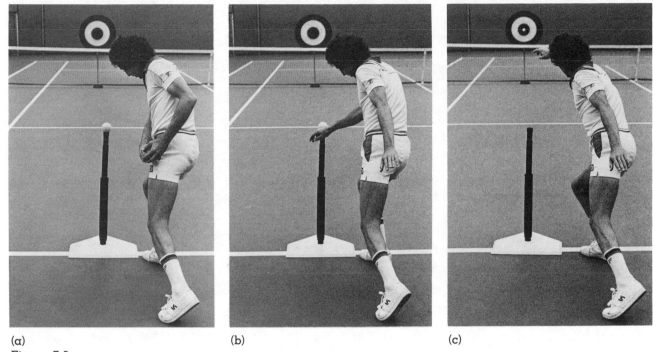

(a)   (b)   (c)

Figure 7-5
Your knuckles should travel in a forward path toward the target (a) before, (b) during, and (c) after contact.

To eliminate all wrist movement, do one or both of the following:

1. *Gently* squeeze the bottom three fingers (pinky, ring, and middle) of your right hand just before, during, and just after contact with the ball. This action will create a firm yet receptive wrist. A firm yet receptive wrist will help to eliminate all wrist movement. After completing the stroke, relax the hand until you are ready to make contact once again.

2. Experience the feeling that you are leading with the pinky knuckles throughout the stroke. This will prevent the strings from producing a circular stroke.

The Arm

The backhand should be a pleasurable experience with the arm and shoulder free of tension and strain. As it extends forward (from a bent to an extended position), the arm should feel long, loose, and relaxed. While creating the stroke the arm should never push, jab, or poke at the ball. At the completion of the stroke, the arm and shoulder should never be straight, locked, rigid, or tense. (See the Stroke Fluidity Section in the Pleasure and Precision Chapter.)

The Shoulder

While the arm is producing the backhand motion, the shoulder should always be in a loose and natural state. At moment of contact, the shoulder should never be tensed. Do *not* try to control your shots by tensing the shoulder. Before, during, and after contact, the shoulder should *not* have any idea of where the ball is going. At moment of contact, the shoulder should be in a pleasurable and ignorant state. Only the pinky knuckle (or knuckles) of the right hand should have "directional control" information.

The Elbow

Try not to focus your attention on the elbow when producing the backhand ground stroke. Focusing your attention too much on the elbow tends to produce a tense and pushy backhand. This type of motion can promote tennis elbow. Focus your attention on the pinky knuckle and shoulder rather than the elbow.

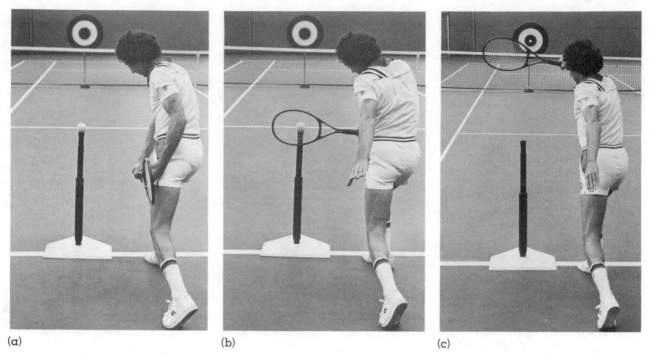

(a)   (b)   (c)

Figure 7-6 a through c
The strings should travel in a forward path toward the target (a) before, (b) during, and (c) after contact.

(d)
Imagine you are throwing your pinky toward your intended target.

DIRECTING A BACKHAND

Now that we have discussed the knuckles, arm, and shoulder, let's see how they can be applied to the pleasure and precision of your backhand.

The Pleasure of a Backhand

When producing a backhand it is most important to receive pleasure in the arm and shoulder. To simulate this experience, place a ball in the hand that usually holds the handle of the racket. Stand with your *right* side to the net, and throw the ball underhand with the knuckles facing the net. This relaxed throwing motion is very similar to a pleasurable and fluid backhand (see Figures 7–4a through c).

The Precision of a Backhand

If you were forced to contact the ball with your knuckles rather than your racket, you would immediately realize that the knuckles would automatically travel in a forward path toward your intended target before, during, and after contact. (See Figures 7–5a through c.) You would immediately realize that the precision of your stroke would be compromised if your knuckles created an excessively circular non-linear motion.

Combining the Pleasure and Precision Principle

Now you are ready to create the backhand stroke with your racket. Because your strings

Figure 7-7
Bring the racket back
before the ball bounces on your side.

SIMPLE ACTIONS TO APPLY TO YOUR CURRENT STROKE

The following section contains simple yet effective *actions* that can immediately be applied to your current backhand stroke.

These same actions are also important elements of the entire full stroke motion that will be introduced in the next section.

Hold the Racket with the Left Finger Pads—"Lefty"

As you are waiting for the ball to be returned, have the left finger pads hold the weight of the racket. This will enable the right hand, arm, and shoulder to remain relaxed and free of tension. The left index finger should touch the strings. Knowing where the strings are before the stroke begins will increase the chances that

Figure 7-8
Just before the opponent contacts the ball, be in the ready alert position.

Figure 7-9
The beginning of the racket backward section.

are just an extension of your knuckles, your strings now need to do the same thing that was just done by your knuckles. The strings should therefore travel in a forward path toward your intended target before, during, and after contact (see Figures 7–6a through c).

Although you are actually hitting the ball, the feeling should be one of throwing your pinky knuckle toward your intended target. It should feel as though the pinky knuckle leaves the body, flies over the net, and lands in the target area. (See Figure 7–6d.) At moment of contact, imagine that your pinky knuckle becomes a tennis ball. Each time you create a stroke, produce a new tennis ball from your pinky knuckle.

To receive additional fluidity, you can imagine that the right shoulder also flies over the net and lands in your intended target area.

proper contact will occur between the ball and the strings. (Refer back to the Senses Chapter.)

The left hand should also help the right hand ·switch immediately to the backhand grip.[1] If it takes you a long period of time to find the correct backhand grip (refer to Grip chapter), then always use the backhand grip when waiting for your opponent to return the ball. If the ball happens to come to your forehand side, you can always switch quickly into the forehand grip.

Bring the Racket Back as Soon as Possible

Bring the racket back—*before* the ball bounces on your side. (See Figure 7–7.) Even when you don't take a full backswing, or when you are running a short distance for the ball, complete the entire backswing *before* the ball lands on your side. Early preparation of the racket will enable you to be prepared to return both slow and very fast moving balls. (Refer to the Racket Backward Section of the Full Forehand Stroke.)

Prolong the Moment of Contact

Try to prolong the moment of contact between the racket and ball by using a fluid pleasurable motion. Trying to prolong the moment of contact will enable you to do the following:

create a stroke with minimal wrist movement.

create a linear section before, during, and after contact.

produce more of a linear and less of a circular follow-forward motion.

AN IN-DEPTH LOOK AT EACH PART OF A FULL BACKHAND STROKE

The following pages contain a detailed breakdown of a simulated backhand tennis stroke. The stroke is broken down into six sections:

1. If you use a two-handed backhand stroke, the left hand would immediately move down the shaft of the racket and join the right hand on the handle of the racket. The entire two-handed backhand stroke will be discussed separately.

BH 1. Racket Ready Alert Position

BH 2. Racket Backward Section

BH 3. Stepping Forward Section

BH 4. Racket Forward Section

BH 5. Linear Contact Section

BH 6. Follow-Forward (Follow-Through) Section

If it is going to make you nervous to look at an in-depth breakdown of the backhand stroke, then just glance at the pictures in this section and go directly to the next part of this chapter— Additional Imagery Actions.

BH 1: Ready Alert Position

Just before your opponent contacts the ball, your racket and body should be in the ready alert position. (See Figure 7–8.) The following functions should be performed while in this position.

1. The racket is out in front of the body and acts as a line that divides the body in half.

2. The left hand ("Lefty") holds almost the entire weight of the racket.

3. The left finger pads receive information about the exact location of the strings and racket and send the information consciously and/or unconsciously to the brain.

4. The right hand, arm, and shoulder are totally loose and natural.

5. The left hand is also waiting to help the right hand to make the necessary grip change.

6. The legs are spread apart and slightly bent. Most of the bending is done from the knees rather than the waist.

7. The weight is equally distributed on the *balls of the feet* (heels are *not* touching the ground).

BH 2: Beginning of the Racket Backward Section

During the racket backward motion, the left hand ("Lefty") immediately performs the following actions:

(a)

(b)

Figure 7-10
The left hand can slightly adjust
the angle of the strings.

(c)

At the completion of the backswing, the *left hand* can *slightly* adjust the angle of the strings (up face, flat face, down face) according to the pattern of your previous backhand strokes. (See Figures 7–10a through c.) Example: If many of your backhand shots are flying too high over the net, have the left hand *slightly* close the face of the racket (down face).

As with the forehand, complete the backswing (regardless of its size) *before* the ball bounces on your side of the court. The only time you might have to abandon this early racket preparation is if you are forced to run full speed to get to a ball.

Figure 7-11
For balance and stroke fluidity,
transfer your weight forward to the right foot.

Starts to bring the racket (strings) around to the left side of the body while helping "Righty" change into the backhand grip. (See Figure 7–9.)

Holds the full weight of the racket as it brings the racket back. (The right arm should feel long and loose. The right shoulder should feel relaxed.)

Completion of the Racket Backward Section

As previously mentioned, the purpose of bringing the racket back is to give additional power to the ball. Therefore, if the approaching ball already has sufficient power (speed), a big backswing isn't as necessary. *Bringing the racket back is a variable*, not a constant.

Figure 7-12
The right hand gently takes the racket away from the left hand.

(a)

(b)

Figure 7-13
Contact should occur
somewhere within the linear contact section.

As the racket is brought back, most of the weight is transferred onto the left foot. If time permits, you can also take a series of small steps that will enable the right hip to turn and directly face the net (picture not shown). At the completion of this turn most of the weight would still be on the left foot.

BH 3: Stepping Forward

To help maintain your balance and to encourage the fluidity of the stroke, transfer your weight forward to your right foot. (See Figure 7–11.)

For anatomical reasons, the moment of contact occurs further in front of the body for the backhand than for the forehand (by several inches). Therefore, you must transfer the weight forward *sooner* when producing a backhand stroke. To be sure that the racket will be in the right position at moment of contact, transfer the weight forward sooner than you think you should (especially when fast balls are approaching).

BH 4: Racket Forward Section

During this section, the racket is brought forward toward the approaching ball.

At the beginning of this section the left hand is stationary and holding the full weight of the racket.

As the right hand starts to move the racket forward, the left hand does *not* let go. Rather, the *right hand gently takes the racket away from the left hand*. (See Figure 7–12.)

(c)

BH 5: Linear Contact Section

Contact should occur somewhere within the linear contact section. The longer the linear section, the more multiple contact options, and the greater the likelihood of producing a consistent and precise tennis stroke. (See Figures 7–13a through c.)

During the linear contact section, the arm begins somewhat bent and extends forward. The handle and strings travel straight toward the intended target with neither the handle nor the strings going ahead of the other. This "tie" between the handle and strings can be accomplished by exaggerating the *feeling* that the *handle* (pinky knuckle) is *leading* the *strings* throughout the entire linear section.

Because the ball must clear the net, the pinky knuckle and racket should complete the

stroke higher than the net. This is accomplished by having the pinky knuckle and racket travel in a gradual low to high linear path.

While it is physically impossible to carry the ball on the strings for an extended period of time, the *feeling* during this section should be one of *prolonged contact between the ball and the strings.*

To improve your balance and stroke fluidity, as the right pinky knuckle is moving forward, the left hand is moving backwards.

BH 6: Follow-Forward (Linear Follow-Through) Section

The linear section of the stroke leads directly into the follow-forward—the final section of the backhand.

In traditional instruction, the motion that

Figure 7-14
The pinky knuckle leads
the other knuckles throughout the stroke.

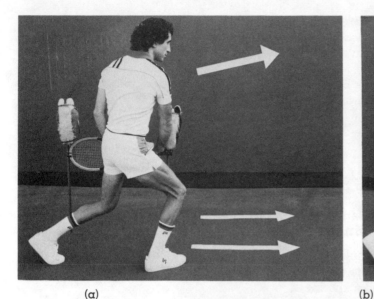

(a)

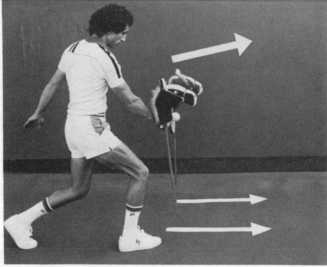

(b)

(c)

Figure 7-15
The string horse should *never* get ahead of the handle horse.

completes the stroke has been called the follow-through. As previously mentioned, the typical backhand follow-through usually contains an excessively circular motion that can jeopardize or eliminate the entire linear contact section. Therefore, to avoid the pitfalls of an excessively circular follow-through, think of this section as the follow-*forward*. Rather than circular fluidity, create *linear fluidity*.

The easiest way to develop a follow-forward motion is to *eliminate all wrist movement* during the linear and follow-forward sections. (See Figure 7–14.)

This can be accomplished by having the *feeling* that the pinky knuckle flows forward toward the net for an extended period of time. Try to get the *feeling* that the pinky knuckle is leading all of the other knuckles throughout the entire stroke. (Refer back to Figure 7–3.)

The follow-forward motion can also be created by *prolonging* the "carrying" sensation during the linear section.

> *Maximize the linear section and eliminate the circular follow-through.*

(a)

(b)

(c)

(d)

Figure 7-16
The full forward path of the racket should create a candy cane.

Figure 7-17
At the completion of the stroke, the birthday card should be facing in the general direction of the target.

ADDITIONAL IMAGERY ACTIONS

The following images will help you to improve the linear and follow-forward sections of a stroke.

Horse Race Image

To create a linear and follow-forward section, it is helpful to imagine that the handle and strings are involved in a horse race. Throughout the entire race it should feel as if string horse *never gets ahead of* handle horse. (See Figures 7–15a through c.) This can be accomplished in two different ways:

   1. Throughout the entire linear and follow-forward sections, it should always *feel* as if *handle horse is winning the race.*

   2. Throughout the entire linear and follow-forward sections, it should *feel* as if both horses are involved in a tie—with both horses running in a dead heat.

Experiment with the above two images and select the one that works best for you.

Candy Cane Image

The full forward path of the racket should create a candy cane as it flows forward. This image will help you to create a linear follow-forward stroke, rather than a circular follow-through stroke. A linear follow-forward will help to guarantee the production of a long linear contact section. (See Figure 7–16.)

   When producing the candy cane remember the following:

Get the feeling that the strings are "carrying" the ball throughout the entire straight section of the cane.

The more power you add to your stroke, the *longer* your candy cane should be.

Let the pinky knuckle or butt of the handle initiate the forward momentum of the racket.

Let the shoulder and arm *naturally* complete the linear follow-forward. *Never* stop the racket to complete the formation of the cane.

The left hand ("Lefty") never lets go of the racket. Rather, the right hand takes the racket away from the left hand.

Tell Your Target "Happy Birthday"

At the completion of the stroke your birthday card should be facing in the *general* direction of your target. (See Figure 7–17.)

Figure 7-18
The handle horse
is always winning the race
along two high horizontal lines.

(a)

(b)

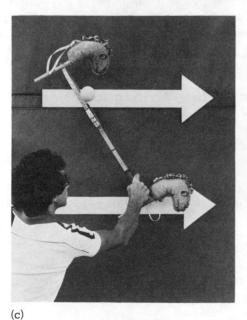

(c)

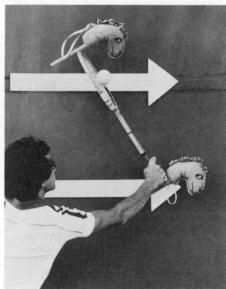

(d)

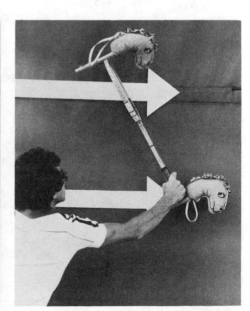

(e)

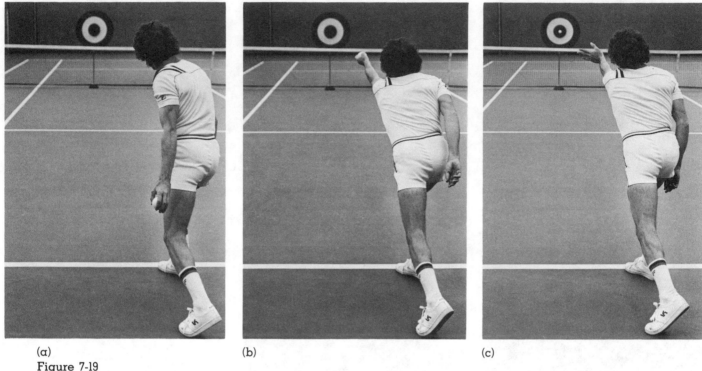

(a)   (b)   (c)

Figure 7-19
Standing with your side to the net, throw the ball underhand.

A HIGH BACKHAND STROKE

Just like the high forehand, this shot should be thought of as a defensive or neutralizing stroke, rather than as an offensive stroke. For this reason, your shot should fly in a high arc over the net and land fairly deeply in your opponent's court.

The high backhand stroke can also be imagined to be a horse race. *Handle horse and string horse race along two high parallel horizontal lines. Handle horse is always winning the race from beginning to end.* This motion will enable the strings to touch on or under the equator of the ball during the entire stroke. (See Figures 7–18a through e.) It is easier to produce this stroke when your side is to the net, and your weight has been transferred onto the front foot. The arm and racket should produce a flowing and gliding forward motion rather than a pushing or punching motion.

Notice that the left hand (not the right) lifts the racket up to the height of the oncoming ball and that handle horse and your right hand remain high in the air throughout the entire stroke.

THE TWO-HANDED BACKHAND STROKE

When a player uses two hands to produce a backhand stroke, it is called a two-handed backhand, a stroke made popular by Jimmy Connors and Chris Evert Lloyd. While the two-handed backhand might at first look difficult, it is actually very similar to the regular forehand stroke.

The Left Hand When Waiting to Use a Two-Handed Backhand

When waiting to use a two-handed backhand, the left finger pads hold the racket in the usual way. As soon as you see that the ball is coming to your backhand, immediately lower the left hand down to the handle. Both left and right hands should now be touching one another.

If you prefer to always have the left hand remain down on the handle (next to the right hand), just remember that your left hand is now not receiving any information as to the exact location and angle of the strings and racket for both backhand and forehand strokes.

(a)   (b)   (c)

Figure 7-20
The left palm should travel in a forward path toward the target (a) before, (b) during, and (c) after contact.

The Left Hand When Using a Two-Handed Backhand

Even though you are a right-handed player, let the left palm become the focal point of the stroke. The left palm directs the ball, "feels" the ball, and energizes the ball. A more precise focal point than the left palm is the "left ball joint" that connects your index finger to your left palm. (If the left palm feels uncomfortable as the focal point, substitute the right pinky knuckle.)

DIRECTING A TWO-HANDED BACKHAND

Pleasure of a Two-Handed Backhand

When producing a two-handed backhand it is most important to receive pleasure in the left arm and left shoulder. To simulate this experience, place a ball in your *left* palm. Stand with your side to the net, and throw the ball underhand. This relaxed throwing motion is very similar to a pleasurable and fluid tennis stroke (see Figures 7–19a through c.)

The Precision of a Two-Handed Backhand

If you were forced to contact the ball with your palm, rather than with your racket, you would immediately realize that the left palm can be the directional focal point of a two-handed backhand. Your left palm would automatically travel in a forward path toward your intended target before, during, and after contact (see Figures 7–20a through c.) You would immediately realize that the precision of your stroke would be compromised if your palm created an excessively circular non-linear motion.

Combining the Pleasure and Precision Principles

Now you are ready to create the two-handed backhand with your racket. Because your strings are just an extension of your palm, your strings now need to do the same thing that was just done by your left palm. The strings should therefore travel in a forward path toward your intended target before, during, and after contact (see Figures 7–21a through c).

(a) (b) (c)

Figure 7-21
The strings should travel in a forward path toward the target (a) before, (b) during, and (c) after contact.

Although you are hitting the ball, the feeling should be one of *throwing* your left palm toward your intended target. *The palm leaves the body, flies over the net, and lands in the target area.*

THE FULL TWO-HANDED BACKHAND STROKE

The pictures in Figures 7–22a through j contain a detailed breakdown of a simulated two-handed backhand stroke. The stroke is once again broken down into six sections.

TBH 1: Racket Ready Alert Position

TBH 2: Racket Backward Section

TBH 3: Stepping Forward Section

TBH 4: Racket Forward Section

TBH 5: Linear Contact Section

TBH 6: Follow-Forward (Follow-Through) Section

Since the two-handed backhand is very similar to a regular forehand stroke, a detailed explanation of each figure will not appear. The most important things to observe in the figures, however, are the following:

Early racket preparation is essential. Notice that the left hand immediately drops down the racket and joins the right hand.

Before, during, and after contact, the racket travels in a linear, low to high path. This enables you to produce a stroke with multiple contact options.

After contacting the ball, there is a linear follow-forward motion rather than a circular follow-through motion.

The ball and strings should *feel* as though they were touching for an extended period of time (carrying motion).

Although it is not shown in these pictures, during the forward path of the racket it is permissible and very often helpful to have the strings lower than the handle.

Advantages of a Two-Handed Backhand

Some players automatically experience more control and comfort when using two hands.

Because two arms are now being used, a physically weaker person (or someone with weak wrists) will usually create stronger strokes.

Some players find it easier to create a longer linear section when using two hands.

Some players find it easier to experience the carrying sensation when using a two-handed backhand.

The right hand can keep the same grip for both forehand and backhand strokes. Only the left hand changes position.

Disadvantages of a Two-Handed Backhand

You cannot reach as far with a two-handed backhand as you can with a one-handed backhand.

Because of your limited reach, you must run a little more to get to the ball.

It is particularly hard to produce a two-handed backhand stroke when the ball is contacted close to the body.

Some players have difficulty executing this stroke when the ball is contacted very close to the ground.

It is sometimes uncomfortable to produce this stroke when contacting the ball above your head.

If, at net, you decide to use a one-handed backhand volley (for greater reach), you may feel awkward with only one hand on the racket.

SUMMARY

The backhand should be a pleasurable physical experience. The arm and shoulder should be free of tension and strain throughout the *entire* stroke.

The racket should be brought back as soon as possible. It should never be brought back more than is necessary.

The pinky knuckle of the right hand directs, feels, and energizes the ball.

Rather than hitting the ball, imagine that you are throwing your pinky knuckle over the net and into your intended target.

Rather than hitting the ball, imagine that the racket is carrying the ball over the net.

The linear contact section should be elongated.

A linear follow-forward motion should be created rather than a circular follow-through motion.

The backhand should contain linear fluidity rather than circular fluidity.

At the completion of most backhands, the pinky knuckle and strings should be at a height higher than the net (due to the height of the net), and pointing in the general direction of the intended target.

Figure 7-22
The full two-handed backhand stroke (a) the ready alert position; (b–d) racket backward section; (e) stepping forward section; (f) racket forward section; (g–i) linear contact section; (j) follow-forward (follow-through) section.

(a)   (b)   (c)

(g)   (h)

(d)

(e)

(f)

(i)

(j)

chapter 8

The Volley

The forehand and backhand strokes that we have already discussed are called ground strokes. (This means that the ball bounces on your side of the court before you contact it.) Sometimes, however, you must contact the ball before it has a chance to bounce on your side. This is referred to as a volley. (See Figure 8–1.)

The closer you are to the net, the greater the likelihood of volleying the ball (assuming your opponent doesn't lob[1] the ball over your head).

In addition to being closer to the net, you will now be closer to your opponent. This means that the ball will reach you much sooner than if you were standing behind the baseline. You will therefore have much less time to prepare for each shot. Because of this crucial time factor, successful volleying strokes are different from ground strokes.

Most of the stroke production and footwork actions introduced in this chapter are designed to maximize your time efficiency. The common theme that pervades most volleying actions (in both singles and doubles) is that *time is of the essence*. Any action that takes too much time to perform should be eliminated from your volleying motion.

SIMPLE ACTIONS TO APPLY TO YOUR CURRENT STROKE

Volley the Ball Over and In

Because the player is close to the net and because the net always looks lower than it really is, too many players neglect to apply the *over and in* concept. They incorrectly try to direct the ball "into," rather than *over and into* their opponent's court. This causes them to incorrectly place the strings on top of the equator of the ball, making the ball land in the net or

shallow in their opponent's court. (Shallow volleys—unless they are well angled—usually put the volleyer in a weak and defenseless position because the opponent can offensively return the ball.)

Even though you are closer to the net, the strings should still contact the ball *under or on the equator* of the ball. It is very dangerous to contact the ball above the equator, unless you are standing extremely close to the net. Remember, the priority is *over and in*.

To help the strings contact under or on the equator, *lead* with the *butt of the handle*. (See Figures 8–2a and b.) Try to get the feeling that the handle is always leading the strings throughout the entire volley. At moment of contact, the handle butt should *feel* like it is closer to the net than the strings. By incorrectly leading with the strings, you will contact the ball above the equator.

Eliminate the Entire Backswing from Your Volley

Because time is of the essence, do not bring the racket back when creating a volley. A backswing wastes a lot of precious time and jeopardizes your accuracy. Moreover, the ball coming toward you usually has sufficient power to make a backswing unnecessary.

The only time to even consider a backswing is when the ball is approaching very slowly. In such a case, a backswing might be necessary in order to generate additional power.

Reach for the Ball with Your Legs, Not Your Arm

When you are playing net, let your legs be the primary stretching source as you reach for the ball. There are two reasons for this:

1. The legs can reach a longer distance than the arm.
2. The further away the arm is from the body, the weaker the arm position and therefore the weaker the shot.

---

1. A lob is a ball that flies high over the net.

Opposite page: Figure 8-1
Making contact with the ball before it bounces on your side of the net is called a volley.

(a)   (b)

Figure 8-2
The handle should feel like it's leading the strings.

Maximizing the Potential Reach

The time factor in the volley generally allows you to take only one step to reach the ball. Therefore, the step that you take needs to be the one that *maximizes* your potential reach.

In the forehand cross-over-and-forward step, the right shoe remains stationary and all reaching is done with the left shoe. (See Figures 8–3, 8–4.) Notice that the stationary anchor foot (the right) and the ball are now both on the right side of the center service line. The moving foot (the left) steps *forward* toward the net as it crosses the right foot.

Notice that the reaching is done with the legs and not with the arm. This will maximize the power and control of your volleys.

In the backhand cross-over-and-forward step, the left shoe now remains stationary and all reaching is done with the right shoe. (See Figure 8–5.) Notice that the stationary anchor foot (the left) and the ball are now both on the

left side of the center service line. The moving foot (the right) steps *forward* toward the net as it crosses the left foot.

Notice once again that the reaching is done with the legs and not with the arm.

How to Feel More Comfortable at the Net

Playing the net can either be heaven or hell. For many players, unfortunately, it is the latter. Here are some helpful hints on how to feel more comfortable while playing the net:

Just *before* your opponent contacts the ball, *stop.* Assume a relaxed and stationary ready alert position *before* your opponent contacts the ball. (Refer back to Figure 8–3.)

Just as your opponent contacts the ball, gently breathe. The entire breath should be *slow* and pleasurable. You should still be breathing as you contact the ball. By

Figure 8-3
The ready alert volley position.

Figure 8-4
The cross-over-and-forward step maximizes your potential reach for a forehand.

Figure 8-5
The cross-over-and-forward step also maximizes your potential reach
for a backhand.

breathing you will keep your body relaxed at moment of contact. (I prefer to breathe in. The receiving of air reminds me that I also want to receive the ball with pleasure rather than muscle it with tension.)

Make believe that the *ball* is actually *yourself* in disguise, not a foreign object that might cause you harm. When the ball approaches you at a fast speed, you are joining yourself very quickly. When it approaches at a slow speed, you are joining yourself very slowly. Every volley gives you the opportunity to meet yourself at net.

Especially in doubles, *hope* that the *ball comes to you.* Look forward to receiving it. Each time the ball does not come to you, feel disappointed rather than relieved.

Using the above techniques can also help you to relax when producing your ground strokes.

FOREHAND VOLLEY

The following pages contain a detailed breakdown of a simulated forehand volley. The stroke is broken down into three sections:

V 1. Racket Ready Alert Position

V 2. Cross-Over-and-Forward Step (Racket Forward Position)

V 3. Linear Contact Section

V 1: Racket Ready Alert Position

While playing the net assume the ready alert position. (See Figure 8–6.) Stand approximately 10 feet away from the net. If you stand closer your opponent's lobs (a high arcing ball) will become too effective.

Feet are spread apart (a wide yet comfortable distance).

Legs are bent. Make sure that most of the bending comes from the legs and not the waist. Good, natural posture (non-rigid) is important.

The weight is evenly distributed on the balls of the feet. The heels are off the ground. (The weight should not be too far forward because if your opponent lobs over your head, there will be no way to recover in time to catch up to the ball.)

Figure 8-6
The ready alert position.

The right arm is bent and relaxed and is out in front of the body (rather than resting at your side). Extending the right arm slightly will help you do this. The right elbow is pointing down.

Because time is of the essence, most advanced players use the same grip (The Continental Grip) for both forehand and backhand volleys. (Refer to the Grip Chapter for pictures and details.)

The ball is coming so fast that they just don't have enough time to change grips. If you intend to become an advanced or tournament player, I would strongly recommend that you learn how to volley using one grip (the Continental Grip).

The problem with the Continental Grip for many people, however, is that the same grip usually does not feel equally comfortable on both sides of the body. For this reason, many players like to change grips.

They use their regular forehand and backhand ground stroke grips when they are at net. They lose some time, but at least they are comfortable with both their forehand and backhand grips. You should experiment and decide for yourself whether to use the same grip or whether to change grips.

V 2: Racket Forward Position and Cross-Over-and-Forward Step

The forward motion of the racket and legs occurs as soon as you see that the ball is coming to the right side of the court. The forward part of the step cuts down the expanding angle of the opponent's ball.

The racket is brought forward, not to the side of the body. The strings are placed in the correct position when the palm is facing the net. (See Figure 8–7.)

The handle slightly leads the strings.

The chest faces the net before contact occurs. This helps prevent any backswing. If the side of your body (left shoulder and hip)

Figure 8-7
The racket forward position and cross-over-and-forward step.

(a)

(b)

Figure 8-8
The linear contact section: (a) first moment of contact;
(b) second moment of contact—arm slightly extended;
(c) completion of linear contact section and forehand volley.

incorrectly faces the net, your racket will automatically be brought back too far.

The right elbow is pointing down and is *in front* (not on the side) *of the body*.

The legs should reach first. Only when the reach of the legs is insufficient should the arm also reach.

As the left leg crosses over and forward, the *left foot* touches the court firmly. If time permits, the weight should be transferred onto the left foot *before* contact occurs.

The back (right) knee is bent.

V 3: Linear Contact Section

From the racket forward position, the linear contact section is produced. Note that the

stroke ends at the completion of the linear contact section. (See Figures 8–8a through c.)

Contact occurs *in front* of the body (not on the side of the body).

Throughout the entire stroke and especially at moment of contact, it should *feel* as though the handle is a little in front of the strings.

As the arm moves forward, it goes from a bent to a *slightly* extended position. Even at the completion of the stroke the arm is never straight or fully extended.

As the racket travels forward it produces a short linear horizontal path.

(c)

BACKHAND VOLLEY

The following pages contain a detailed break-down of a simulated backhand volley. The stroke is broken down into three sections:

V 1. Racket Ready Alert Position

V 2. Cross-Over-and-Forward Step (Racket Forward Position)

V 3. Linear Contact Section

BV 1: Racket Ready Alert Position

The ready alert position is the same for the backhand volley as it is for the forehand volley. (See Figure 8–9.)

If you need to refresh your memory, review the forehand ready alert position in the previous section.

BV 2: Racket Forward Position and Cross-Over-and-Forward Step

The forward motion of the racket occurs as soon as you see that the ball is coming to the left side of the court. The "forward" part of the step cuts down the expanding angle of the opponent's ball. (See Figure 8–10.)

The left hand brings the racket forward and prevents the strings from moving backwards. It also holds the full weight of the racket.

The left hand (strings) and right shoulder are approximately the same distance away from the net. There is no backswing.

The handle is in front of the strings.

When the linear section begins, the right hand *takes* the racket away from the left hand. The left hand does *not* drop or let go of the racket.

After the racket is taken away from the left hand, the *left* arm extends and moves backwards (for balance).

For anatomical reasons, contact occurs farther out in front of the body with the backhand volley than with the forehand volley.

The butt of the handle should *feel* as though it were leading the strings throughout the entire linear section.

The pinky knuckle also directs the backhand volley. Therefore, whenever possible the pinky knuckle should be higher than the net at the completion of the stroke. *The ball follows the path of the pinky.*

To achieve backhand volley fluidity, imagine you are *throwing* the pinky over the net and into the desired target area, rather than trying to hit the ball over the net and into the desired target area. As you throw

Figure 8-9
The ready alert position.

The legs should reach first. Only when the reach of the legs is insufficient should the arm also reach.

As the right leg crosses over and forward, the entire right foot touches the court firmly. The weight is transferred onto the right foot before contact occurs.

The back (left) knee is bent.

BV 3: Linear Contact Section

From the racket forward position, the linear contact section is produced. (See Figures 8–11a through c.) Note that the stroke ends at the completion of the linear contact section.

Figure 8-10
Racket forward position
and cross-over-and-forward step.

(a)

(b)

Figure 8-11
The linear contact section:
(a) first moment of contact;
(b) second moment of contact;
(c) completion of linear contact section
    and backhand volley.

(c)

Figure 8-12
The volley is similar to
a catching motion.

Figure 8-13
Catch the ball
in your racket.

the pinky, it should feel as if the pinky were leading the strings throughout the *entire* stroke.

Prolong contact between the ball and strings as the arm extends forward.

Note that the arm extends farther with the backhand volley than with the forehand volley. Even when the right arm fully extends, however, it is not locked or stiff; though extended, it is never rigid.

IMAGERY ACTIONS FOR THE MOST IMPORTANT ELEMENTS OF THE STROKE

The Volley Arm Motion— Catch the Ball

Most players lack precision and consistency on the volley because they think of it as a power stroke and utilize a punching, jabbing, thrusting, or attacking motion.

If your volleys are inconsistent, slow down and shorten your forward stroke until you can consistently contact the ball. Eliminate all backswing and follow-through. You can do this by simply moving your racket forward and placing the strings in the path of the oncoming ball.

The volley arm motion most resembles a *catching motion*. (See Figure 8–12.) When you catch a ball your arm remains bent and in front of your body throughout the entire catch. *Your arm never moves backward.*

The Volley Arm Motion— Catch the Ball in Your Racket

To apply this catching motion to your volleys, make believe that your racket is a butterfly net. (See Figure 8–13.) At moment of contact, *feel* as if you were catching the tennis ball in the net. Just have patience and wait for the ball's arrival. By going out to meet the ball (by extending the arm too much), you will jeopardize the precision of the volley.

Figure 8-14
The strings are a backboard.

Figure 8-15
The forward path of the racket should resemble
a gentle linear or tubular section.

Forehand volley

(a)

(b)

Backhand volley

(c)

(d)

(a)   (b)

Figure 8-16
Contacting the ball above your head: (a) the high forehand volley; (b) the high backhand volley.

When you come to net, think of yourself as a baseball player rather than a tennis player. Make believe that you and your opponent are on the same team: he throws the ball and you catch it.

The Strings Are a Backboard

Instead of believing that you are catching the ball in the racket, you can imagine that the racket is a backboard (or trampoline). Just put the backboard in the path of the ball and the ball will do the rest. Notice that at moment of contact the bottom of the board is closer to the net than the top of the board. The bottom of the backboard represents the handle of the racket and the top of the backboard represents the strings. This "handle first" relationship helps to

insure that the ball will fly over the net. (See Figure 8–14.)

The Tubular Volley

Once your volleys become more consistent, you can begin to bring the racket forward. The forward path of the racket should resemble a gentle linear or tubular section. For anatomical reasons, the forehand linear section is shorter than the backhand linear section. (See Figures 8–15a through d.)

Exercise to Eliminate the Backswing

If your volley has a big backswing, you will need to retrain yourself in order to eliminate or minimize it. Attach a piece of rope to the top of the racket and tie it around the top of the net. Stand sufficiently far away from the net so that it would be impossible to bring the racket back any further. From this position create a cross-over-and-forward step. Notice that the rope will permit the racket to be moved forward but not back. Repeating this drill many times will train the body to eliminate any backswing.

CONTACTING THE BALL AT DIFFERENT HEIGHTS

Contacting the Ball Above Your Head

Even on high forehand and backhand volleys, the *handle leads the strings*. (See Figures 8–16a–b.) The height of the obstacle, the net, must still be respected. The first fraction of a second the strings touch the ball, contact occurs *under or on the equator*. Touching under or on the equator will at least guarantee that the ball flies *over the net*. If the ball flies too far over the net (flies long), contact the ball less under and more on the equator.

The High Smash Volley (An Offensive, Highly Energized Volley)

To smash a volley that is returned above your head, you must *feel* that the strings are contacting two areas of the ball before the ball leaves the strings. First, *feel* as if the strings were touching a little underneath the equator. (This will only be possible if the handle leads the strings.) Then, with a loose hand and wrist, permit the strings to flop forward (moving in front of the handle), creating the feeling that you are now touching the ball on top of the equator. Just before, during, and just after contact, the feeling of this stroke should resemble a flat service motion. If the ball is going long, lead less with the handle.

Having the strings touch at least a little under the equator each time will guarantee that the ball will go over the net. Having the strings next *feel* as though they are touching above the equator will then help the ball to go into the court.

Make sure that the wrist and fingers are "loose as a goose" during moment of contact. When performing this stroke correctly, you will *feel* totally out of control. Total looseness of the wrist, however, will lead to total control.

Lead with the handle first and then let the wrist feel like a loose hinge. Let the momentum of the racket itself create the power. Do not squeeze the fingers or try to add any type of force. At moment of contact, the momentum of the racket, not you, hits the smash. Sometimes it will *almost* feel as though the racket were about to fly out of your hand. Don't worry about this feeling—it means you are on the right track.

Figure 8-17
The racket creates a horizontal path as the strings sand under the equator of the tennis ball.

(a)

(b)

Contacting the Ball
Below the Level of the Net

Volleying the ball below the height of the net is difficult, usually resulting in a ball that flies into the net rather than over it. Here are some hints to help you volley a ball when it is low:

Recognize that your volley will be a defensive one. Do not try to produce a powerful and offensive stroke from this position.

Change the usual *over* and *in* priority into *up, over* and *in*. When the ball leaves your strings, its path must first be directly *UP* in the air (like a space ship), then *over* the net, and then *into* your opponent's court.

For you to achieve this *up* priority, at moment of contact with the ball your strings must be almost totally open (up face racket). Regardless of whether it is a forehand or backhand volley, the strings must now touch way underneath the equator (close to the South Pole of the ball).

The closer you are to the net, the more you should focus your attention on this *UP* priority.

Remember to bend from the knees and not the waist.

REFINEMENTS

Backspin Volleys

Intermediate and advanced players should also be able to produce forehand and backhand volleys with backspin. (As the ball flies over the net, it has a backward rotation. Refer to the chapter on Spins for a more detailed explanation.) The backspin volley is very versatile, giving the player increased control. It can be used to produce aggressive strokes as well as gentle strokes (called finesse backspins).

To create a backspin volley, imagine you are sanding the material off the lower half of the ball. This sanding motion creates friction that causes the ball to spin backwards. The more backward spin you desire, the further below the equator the strings should "sand" the ball. (See Figures 8–17a and b.)

Principles to follow when sanding:

Do not use an excessive wrist motion to sand the ball.

Feel as though you are leading with the handle *throughout* the entire sanding motion.

Feel as if the ball were staying on the strings for a long period.

The strings should remain at the same height (on the same horizontal path) throughout the entire sanding motion. The strings do *not* start off high and end low. A high to low chopping motion will cause the ball to go into the net or to land too shallow in your opponent's court.

SUMMARY

The volley is an *over* and *in* stroke. For you to consistently produce this over and in stroke, the strings should always touch on or under the equator of the ball.

Initiating each stroke by leading with the handle will help produce an over and in stroke.

The racket and hand move forward. Eliminate the backswing from your volley motion.

When volleying, reach first with the legs. A cross-over-and-forward step will maximize your reach.

Because time is of the essence, wait for the ball with arms in front of the body rather than on the side of the body.

When extending the arm, the hand and racket move on a linear, *horizontal path*.

During the volley, the arm extends more on the backhand than on the forehand.

chapter 9

The Serve

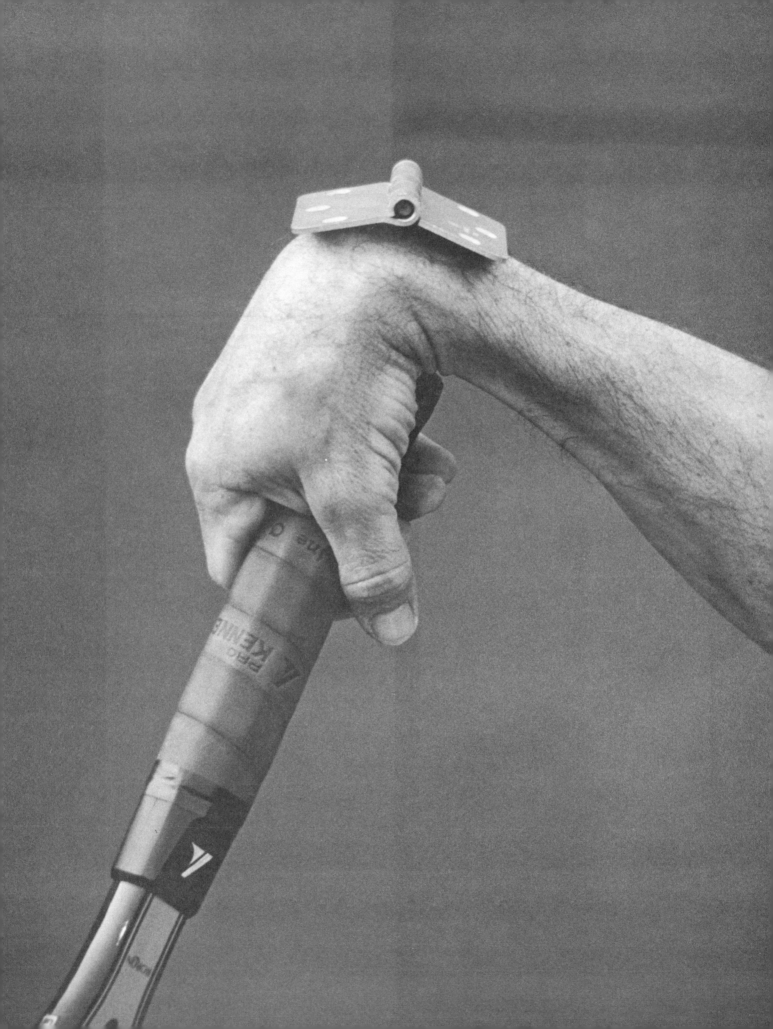

The serve is the stroke that begins each point. If you cannot begin a point, you can never win a point, game, set, or match. For this reason many competitive players consider the serve to be the most important stroke.

The priorities of producing a serve are similar to the priorities of producing any other stroke: the ball must first fly *over* the net, and then land *in* the appropriate service box—the one diagonally across from you. The purpose of this chapter is to isolate some of the components of these important service actions. As soon as you understand these actions, your serve will become more consistent and precise. These actions will also help you make corrections when your serve is not working well.

What makes the serve difficult to produce is the limited size of the service box compounded by its adjacency to the net. Whereas for all other strokes, your target area is 100 percent of your opponent's side, in the serve your target area—the service box—is only about 27 percent.

In actuality, the target area is even smaller, because the part of the service box closest to you is blocked by the net. (If the net were only an inch high, it would be possible for you to serve into the whole service box.) Thus, due to the height of the net, the available service area is only about half of the service box—a mere 13½ percent of your opponent's side.

Because of the high obstacle and the small target area, the serve is more of a precision stroke than it is a power stroke. Therefore, power should be the last ingredient added to the serve.

CONSISTENCY

A consistent serve is the key to tennis. The rules of tennis, however, have unintentionally encouraged people to have inconsistent serves, because players are given two chances to get the ball over the net and into the correct service box. Many players, therefore, take the first serve too lightly. They use too much power

and muscle and not enough pleasure and precision. On the second serve they tend to use too much gentleness and tension and not enough pleasure and precision. The stakes are too low on the first serve and too high on the second. There is no middle ground.

Your service goal for the next year should be to slow down the speed of your first serve and increase the speed of your second serve. Both serves should contain a reasonable amount of speed and a lot of pleasure and precision.

FLAT AND SPIN SERVES

There are basically two types of service motions—the flat serve and the spin serve.

In the flat serve the ball has a minimal amount of spin as it flies *low* over the net and into the diagonal service box, whereas in the spin serve the ball has a lot of spin as it flies *high* over the net and into the diagonal service box.

Since the easier and more natural serve for most players is the flat serve, it will be discussed first. The spin serve (usually used as the second serve by most tournament players) will be discussed later on in the Spin Serve Section.

Once again, please remember that many of these simulated pictures represent what the stroke should *feel* like rather than the actual physical realitites of stroke production.

PRACTICING THE SERVE

Serving is like a totally different sport, similar in motion only to the overhead smash. Because it is not similar to a forehand or backhand, it must be practiced separately. Unfortunately, most players never practice their serves, yet they always expect their serves to be reliable. If you don't practice the *sport of serving*, it is silly to get upset with yourself when you double fault (that is, miss two opportunities to get the serve into the target area). If you consider yourself a serious tennis player, you should

Opposite page: **Figure 9-1**
Your wrist should feel like a weak, well-oiled, floppy hinge.

 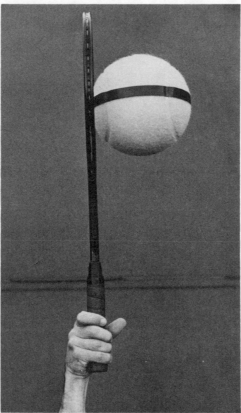 

(a)   (b)   (c)

Figure 9-2
The over-and-in moment of contact feeling: (a) over, (b) and, (c) in.

own a bucket of tennis balls (they can be old) and you should practice your serve a *minimum* of five minutes a week. If you do not practice the serve, chances are that your serve will remain on the same level indefinitely.

Even if you just practice your regular serve—regardless of how primitive it is—the consistency of your serve will improve. But if you practice the *specific* service actions in this chapter, the consistency of your serve will improve much faster.

SIMPLE, EFFECTIVE IMAGERY ACTIONS FOR YOUR CURRENT SERVE

Improving the Precision of the Serve

The most important part of the body used in producing the serve is the *wrist*. The correct wrist motion can make up for a poor ball toss,

improper grip, poor racket motion, or incorrect body position. Proper wrist motion will determine proper contact between the ball and strings. If you have always suffered from an inconsistent serve, focus your attention on developing what is called the "wrist snap."

The wrist snap is a very elusive skill to acquire because it has been improperly labeled. When most people hear the phrase "snap the wrist," they believe that some extra work must be done by the wrist in order to snap it. Many players—particularly men—incorrectly tighten the wrist (by squeezing the handle with their fingers when trying to snap the wrist).

Rather than being tight or stiff at moment of contact, the wrist should feel like a weak, well-oiled, floppy hinge. (See Figure 9–1.) It should be "loose as a goose."

A loose "hinge" will allow the racket to flop forward. In other words, if a player wants more control (and more power), paradoxically he must do less with the fingers and wrist, not more.

If you correctly serve the ball with a loose wrist, you will *feel* as though you have no control or power. Do not be worried by this feeling. If you practice enough, these free and out-of-control feelings will eventually lead to a powerful and controlled serve. (Of course, you must be sure that the fingers are not too loose, or the racket will fly out of your hand.)

A loose wrist is created by doing any one or more of the following:

Keeping the fingers of the right hand loose and semi-relaxed at moment of contact with the ball.

Moving the right hand all the way down to the end of the handle. You can even try serving with the pinky extending off the butt of the handle of the racket, with only four fingers holding the racket.

Pretending that all the fingers of the right hand (except the thumb) are lightly glued together.

Producing the Over-and-In Motion

Most players have a misconception about the serve that causes them to continually hit the ball into the net. They think they must contact the ball above the equator in order to have a successful serve. They incorrectly try to serve the ball "into" the service box, rather than over *and in.*

In order for you to have a successful serve, the strings must contact either on or a little under the equator of the ball. This will at least permit the ball to first fly *over* the net.

"Over." Leading with the butt of the handle will guarantee that the strings first touch *on or under the equator.* (See Figure 9–2a.) This will help the ball clear the net. (Note that if the strings touch too far under the equator, the ball will fly long.)

"And." The floppy wrist permits the strings to start moving forward. When the strings contact the equator of the ball you will experience a feeling of power. (See Figure 9–2b.)

"In." Just before the ball leaves the strings, you should *feel* as though the strings were touching *on top of the equator.* (See Figure 9–2c.) This feeling will help the ball land within the service box. A *loose* wrist (created by loose and relaxed fingers), will help to produce the feeling of in.

The over-and-in concept represents the player's *"sensation"* of what is happening. Even though at moment of contact the strings cannot possibly touch all three areas of the ball, it should *feel* as if they were.

Figure 9-3
Lower the strings before contacting the ball.

(a)   (b)

Figure 9-4
Keep the feet stationary to improve the consistency in your serve.

Improving the Power of Your Serve

Every player has a different service motion. Regardless of your personal style of serving, however, there is still a "common ground" that all tennis rackets should pass through during the service motion. Before the player contacts the ball, the strings should be lowered behind you. Lowering the strings before they travel up to contact the ball helps to transmit a lot of power to the ball. If you don't receive enough power from your serve, your strings have probably not gone far enough down before returning up to meet the ball above your head.

The best way to check the path of your racket is to have a friend watch you serve. Let her/him check to see how far down your strings travel before going up to meet the ball. You can become accustomed to lowering the strings by doing the following: *Start* the entire service motion with the strings already lowered. This position is referred to as the Half Service Position.

Make believe that there is a paint brush attached to the end of your racket. Before you toss the ball in the air, dip the "racket paint brush" into the paint barrel. (See Figure 9–3.)

Dipping the brush into the can forces the strings to begin the serve from the Half Service Position.

Starting from this position does the following:

increases the power of your serve,

forces you into concentrating more on the arm and wrist motion,

increases your accuracy (because the body needs to coordinate fewer actions).

Figure 9-5
Serving from the right side of the court.

Improving Consistency

Having the feet in motion during the serve usually interferes with the precision of the serve. Therefore, to improve the consistency and precision of the serve, *keep the feet stationary throughout the entire serve.* At first, not moving the feet will feel very restrictive and awkward. Eventually, however, you will feel balanced and your serve will become more consistent.

While in this stationary position, you may initially feel that you are losing power. This is an illusion. You can serve a ball with great power without ever moving the feet. The *shoulder, arm, hips, and knees* as well as the momentum of the racket supply most of the power when serving.

If you feel you must move your feet, then just move one. Let the back foot (right) step forward just *after* you contact the ball. The *toe* of the left (front) foot, however, should remain stationary throughout the entire serve. Even on

skis, you should be able to remain balanced and stationary throughout the entire service motion. (See Figures 9–4a and b.)

Improving the Positioning of Your Body

Set your left shoe at a 45 degree angle to the baseline regardless of which side of the court you are serving from. (See Figure 9–5.)

If an arrow were placed on the ground and if it were touching both the left and the right shoes, the arrow should be pointing in the direction of your intended target (the service box diagonally across from you). (See Figure 9–6.)

Improving Your Toss

While a good toss does not guarantee that your serve will be good, an accurate toss certainly helps the serving process. Tossing a ball in the

Figure 9-6
Serving from the right side of the court.

Figure 9-7
Palming the ball for the serve.

air using an underhand motion is a very simple action. What usually makes tossing uncomfortable and difficult to perform is the fact that we must use an untrained throwing arm to do it. Outside of tennis we never need to precisely toss a ball with our weaker arm.

To improve your toss, practice the motion when you are not playing tennis—for example, while watching television or while on the telephone. Toss the ball up in the air underhand, and catch it in your left palm.

Palm the Ball Up a Shaft

A lot of players incorrectly hold the ball with the tips of their fingers before tossing it in the air. This causes excessive wrist motion, which leads to inconsistent tossing. Instead, use the palm more and the ends of the fingers less when tossing the ball up in the air. As you gently toss the ball up, you should feel as though you were "palming" it straight up a shaft. (See Figure 9–7.)

More "tossing" information will appear later in this chapter.

The Service Grip

The most versatile service grip is the Continental Forehand Grip. It allows you the options to produce both flat and spin serves. If you intend to become an advanced or tournament player, I would strongly recommend that you learn how to serve using the Continental Forehand Grip. (Refer to the Grip chapter for pictures and details.)

The problem with the Continental Grip for many players, however, is that it requires many service repetitions in order to learn how to produce both a flat and spin serve. The wrist and arm are placed in an uncomfortable posi-

Opposite page: Figure 9-8
When producing a flat serve, you should feel as if you were hammering the ball.

Figure 9-9
Service ready position.

tion, especially when producing a flat serve. Most people don't have the time or interest to do the needed repetitions in order to feel comfortable serving with the Continental Forehand Grip.

For this reason, most people serve using an Eastern Forehand Grip. The main advantage of an Eastern Forehand Grip is that the flat serves are very easy to produce. The main disadvantage of an Eastern Forehand Grip is that spin serves are *very* difficult to produce.

You should experiment and decide for yourself whether to use a Continental or Eastern Forehand Grip.

THE FULL SERVICE MOTION

The full service motion will now be discussed. By using simulated service pictures, we are able to isolate the most important sections of the full service motion.

The most important areas to observe in the full service motion are the following:

a. The feet are stationary throughout the serve.
b. The left side is facing the net for an extended period of time.
c. The tossing arm remains high in the air for a long time.
d. The strings are lowered behind you before they are raised to contact the ball.

If any of this information gets too detailed for you, don't get psyched-out. Just add one new action at a time to your current serve (regardless of how primitive you feel it is). Practice that new action until your body performs it automatically.

Note: Due to the camera angle, the height

Figure 9-10
The racket drop.

of the tossed ball will appear to be a little higher than is actually necessary.

THE FLAT SERVE

The type of serve that we will be looking at first is called the flat serve.

Characteristics

When a served ball is contacted solidly by the strings it is called a flat serve. The server focuses his attention on transmitting power (as opposed to spin) onto the ball. The following are characteristics of the flat serve:

    a. The ball has minimal spin as it flies over the net.

    b. The ball clears the net by only a small margin. (A large margin would cause it to fly past the intended service box.)

    c. The path of the ball will appear to be a straight line, but in fact, it is a slightly curved line.

Purpose

The purpose of a flat serve varies depending on your tennis level.

    a. The purpose of a beginner's flat serve is to start the point.

    b. The purpose of a tournament player's flat serve to start the point in such a way as to force the opponent into returning the ball defensively, or to prevent him from returning the ball at all.

Sensation of Producing a Flat Serve—Hammering

When a hammer hits a nail squarely, the body receives a powerful, solid sensation. This feeling is very similar to the vibration felt in the arm and hand when correct contact is made between the strings and the ball during a flat serve. To experience this sensation, make believe the racket is the hammer and the ball is the nail. At moment of impact, the hammer (strings) must make solid contact with the nail (ball). (See Figure 9–8.)

    The *momentum of the racket*, rather than tension and muscle, provides the needed energy.

AN IN-DEPTH LOOK AT EACH PART OF A FULL SERVICE MOTION

In this section, the serve will be broken down into nine parts:

    SRV 1. The Service Ready Position
    SRV 2. The Racket Drop
    SRV 3. The Scarecrow Extended Arm Motion
    SRV 4. The Ball Release
    SRV 5. Lowering the Strings
    SRV 6. Raising the Strings
    SRV 7. Contact
    SRV 8. Post-Contact
    SRV 9. Completion of the Serve

SRV 1: Service Ready Position

Take your time before beginning to serve. Relax. Bouncing a ball and/or taking a deep breath will help you to accomplish this. Take advantage of the fact that you do not have to begin the service motion until *you* are ready. (See Figure 9–9.)

Figure 9-11
The scarecrow extended arm motion.

The wrist, fingers, arm and shoulder of the right arm are semi-extended and limp.

The left finger pads hold the full weight of the racket.

The knees are slightly bent.

The left toe is solidly planted just behind the baseline. A 45 degree angle is created between the left shoe and the baseline.

The weight is evenly distributed.

SRV 2: The Racket Drop

Once the service motion begins, the strings never fully stop although they might slow down. Keeping the racket in motion should be a pleasurable experience. Your body should be in a tensionless state. (See Figure 9–10.)

The server gently lets the racket head fall.

The left palm *slowly* starts to rise toward the sky with the ball still in it.

The left (front) leg bends a little more as the weight of the body is gradually transferred onto it.

The entire right arm is still loose, relaxed and free.

SRV 3: The Scarecrow Extended Arm Motion

The head of the racket (strings) acts like the end of a *very slow* moving pendulum as it swings back and up. (See Figure 9–11.)

The wrist, fingers, arm and shoulder of the right arm remain loose.

The right and left arms both extend slightly and travel up to a "scarecrow" arm position.

The racket is pointing toward the back fence.

The weight has now been transferred onto the left leg and remains in this position throughout the rest of the serve.

SRV 4: The Ball Release

The ball should be released at eye level or above. The left hand must calculate how high the ball needs to be tossed in order for the constantly moving racket to eventually contact it. (This synchronization process only occurs after *many* practice serves.)

Figure 9-12
The ball release.

After the ball is released, the tossing arm should remain high in the air for an extended period of time. (See Figure 9–12.) This action will keep the left shoulder higher than the right. A "higher" left shoulder will make it easier for the strings to touch on or a little under the equator of the ball. (By lowering the left shoulder too soon, you increase the chances that the strings will touch the ball above the equator, sending it into the net.)

The left palm releases the ball at eye level (or a little above).

The left hand and arm extend farther up, as though the left palm were reaching up to check for rain drops.

The wrist and fingers of the right hand continue to remain loose throughout this stage.

(a)

(b)

Figure 9-13
Lowering the strings.

The swinging momentum of the racket and a tensionless shoulder *slowly* swing the racket higher.

The right arm begins to bend as it slowly swings the racket higher.

SRV 5: Lowering the Strings

Let the racket almost drop down by itself. Power, muscle, and/or tension should *not* be used. (See Figures 9–13a and b.)

The wrist and fingers of the right hand continue to remain loose.

Gravity and the slow and gentle momentum of the racket cause the strings to drop slowly.

The left arm and palm still remain high in the air.

SRV 6: Raising the Strings

The racket should not stop as it is lowered and raised. (See Figures 9–14a and b.) The head of the racket has built up a soothing, gentle momentum throughout all the previous stages. (Stopping the head of the racket when it is lowered would compromise the rhythm and momentum gained in the first five stages.)

The handle butt leads the strings. The arm extends as the butt of the handle moves up to the sky and forward.

The wrist, fingers, and right shoulder remain loose and free.

The shoulder adds pleasurable energy to the momentum of the racket. Be careful that the fingers do *not* squeeze the handle.

The left (tossing) arm and palm begin slowly to fall.

(a)

(b)

Figure 9-14
Raising the strings.

The left front leg begins to extend as the right arm brings the racket toward the ball.

Think of the left front leg (rather than the right shoulder) as your power source. If you want more power, bend the left (and right) leg more so that your body can add more power to the ball as your left leg extends.

SRV 7: Contact

It is vital that the wrist and fingers of the right hand remain loose and free throughout the entire contact period. When the wrist is "hinging" correctly, you will feel that you have given up control and power. Stay with this seeming loss of control and power so that a new level of mastery can be born out of *pleasure*, not muscle or tension.

At moment of contact, the right arm is extended but not stiff, rigid, or locked.

The strings *first contact* the ball on or *a little under the equator*. This is accomplished by having the handle lead the strings into contact. (See Figure 9–15a.)

As the wrist loosely flops forward, the strings will *feel* as though they were contacting the ball above the equator, however this should occur *after* the strings contact on or a little under the equator. (See Figures 9–15b and c.)

The body remains stationary and fully balanced throughout the entire contact period.

(a)

(b)

(c)
Figure 9-15
The wrist and fingers should feel loose
and free throughout the contact period:
(a) first contact; (b) second contact; (c) third contact.

SRV 8: Post-Contact

At this moment you will have no idea of where the ball is going. You will once again have a feeling of "loss of control." (See Figure 9–16.)

> The wrist and fingers still remain loose and free.
>
> The body is still stationary and fully balanced.

SRV 9: Completion of the Serve

The serve is finished at the completion of this motion. The racket is stationary only at the beginning and at the end of the serve.

> The wrist and fingers continue to remain loose and free.
>
> The momentum of the racket causes the loose wrist to flop over into a goose neck position. (See Figure 9–17a.)
>
> The right arm falls and crosses over to the left side of the body. (See Figure 9–17b.)
>
> The body is stationary and balanced.

Figure 9-16
At the moment of post-contact,
you will have a feeling of loss of control.

THE BALL TOSS

Placing the Toss for the Flat Serve

If the ball were tossed correctly and permitted to fall, it would land somewhere within the round target area, six to twelve inches in front of the shoe or baseline and to the right of the lead (left) shoe. (See Figure 9–18.)

A correct ball toss will enable you to:

> Use the power from your body most efficiently.
>
> Contact the ball on or a little *under* the equator with the greatest amount of consistency.
>
> Maintain your balance throughout the entire serve.

If you prefer to have the right foot step onto the court after moment of contact, your ball toss can be a little farther forward.

CORRECTIONS FOR THE SERVE

Serve Is Going into the Net

When the ball flies into the net, this means that the strings incorrectly contacted the ball on top of the equator. The following corrections contain physical actions that will enable the strings to touch on or a little under the equator of the ball.

> Lead more with the butt of the handle just before contacting the ball.
>
> Toss the ball closer to the body (not too close, however).
>
> Toss and contact the ball higher in the air.
>
> Leave the tossing hand and arm in the air for a longer period of time after the ball

(a)

(b)

Figure 9-17
Completion of the serve.

leaves the hand. This will keep the left shoulder raised higher than the right, which will help the racket to contact the ball on or under the equator.

Imagine that the net is twice as high as it really is.

Serve Is Going Long (Past the Service Box)

When the ball flies past the service box, this means that the strings contacted the ball too much underneath the equator. The following corrections contain physical actions that will enable the strings to touch on or a little under the equator of the ball.

Have the strings contact the ball more nearly on the equator rather than under it.

To overcompensate, you might have to imagine that the strings are touching a little above the equator. This is a very dangerous image, however, and should be used only to overcompensate. If, in fact, your strings really do touch above the equator, your serve will fly into the net.

Relax your fingers at moment of contact, enabling your wrist to loosen up even more. A loose wrist will encourage the strings to contact the ball on or closer to the equator.

Toss the ball a little lower.

Step back, away from the baseline toward the back fence. (This technique should only be used during a competitive emergency situation, not as a permanent solution.)

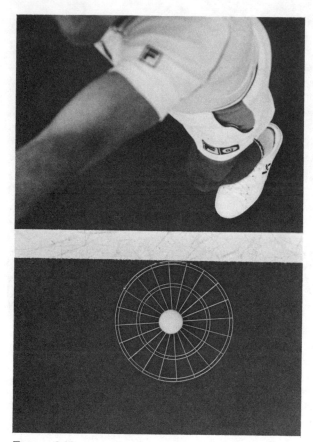

Figure 9-18
The toss for the flat serve.

THE SPIN SERVE

Now that we have looked at the flat serve in detail, we're ready to look at the second type of serve, the spin serve.

Whenever a served ball revolves many times per second, it is called a spin serve. The server focuses his attention on the number of revolutions of the ball, as opposed to the speed of the ball.

Just as much power and fluidity are used for the spin serve as the flat serve. The results, however, happen to be different.

Characteristics

The ball spins many times per second as it flies over the net.

A spin serve tends to travel slower than a flat serve.

The path of the ball should resemble a high arc.

A sophisticated spin serve will clear the net by a margin of several feet.

The spin of the ball pulls the ball down, causing it to land inside the service box.

Most right-handed spin serves move to the left (from the server's perspective) after they bounce.

Purpose

A correctly executed spin serve, since it has high clearance of the net and spin, will fly over the net and *into* the service box with a certain reassuring frequency.

Sensation of Spinning the Ball— Sanding

A tennis ball is composed of two substances, rubber and cloth. In order for the ball to spin, a *friction*-oriented motion must take place between the *strings* and the *cloth*. The easiest way to create this friction is to imagine you are *de-fuzzing* (sanding) the cloth off the ball. The spin serve maximizes focus on the cloth and minimizes focus on the rubber. A flat serve maximizes focus on the rubber (by hammering the ball) and minimizes attention on the cloth. *Hammering produces speed; sanding produces spin.*

TRY TO PROLONG THE SANDING SENSATION FOR AS LONG AS POSSIBLE.

HOW TO PRODUCE A SPIN SERVE

To spin the ball, the server must imagine that sandpaper has replaced his strings. His goal is to totally *de-fuzz* each *ball under the equator*. (See Figure 9–19.) The strings sand the cloth, not the rubber. The friction of this sanding action will cause the ball to spin.

As with the flat serve, the shoulder and arm should be relaxed, rather than tensed, when the strings contact the ball. Make sure that you are not stopping the racket (as you contact the ball) in order to produce this type of serve. To prevent yourself from stopping the racket, make sure your fingers and wrist are always relaxed. This will encourage the racket to be in constant motion throughout the serve.

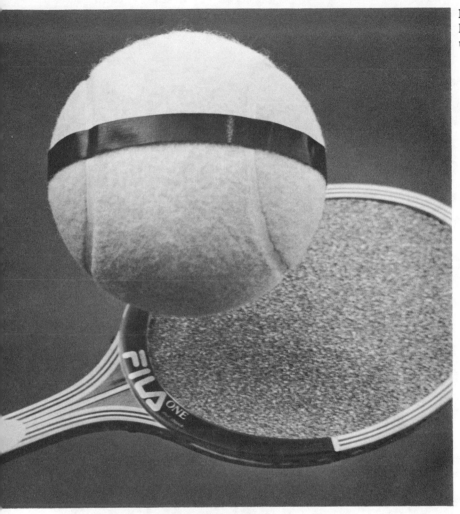

Figure 9-19
De-fuzz the material
under the equator.

The Exaggerated High Arc of the Spin Serve

To create a high arcing sidespin or topspin serve, the player must try to program the ball to first fly *directly up*, by sanding well underneath the equator of the ball. After the ball has been sanded *up*, the arc and spin of the ball will automatically cause the ball to fly *over* the net and *into* the desired service box.

The notion of sanding the ball up in the air sounds easy enough. In reality it isn't. The body will usually reject this physical concept. You see the service box; it is diagonally *over* on the other side of the net. You see the opponent; he is also *over* on the other side of the net. Therefore, the body will try to sand the ball *over* the net. The body will do almost anything but allow you the freedom to *sand the ball up,*

up, up. The racket's path, like that of the ball, is up. The server must forget that there is a court, a net, a service box, and an opponent.

To help produce a spin serve, imagine you are *sanding yourself a pop fly* (a pop fly ball in baseball goes vertically up). You can also imagine that you are sanding the ball *up* an elevator shaft.

Here is a helpful "sanding up" exercise. Leave the tennis court and stand five to six feet away from the fence. Next, try to sand the ball up, over, and into the tennis court. Unless your strings sand way underneath the equator of the ball, the ball will never clear the fence.

Contact During a Spin Serve

It is vital that the fingers, wrist, arm, and shoulder remain loose and free before, during,

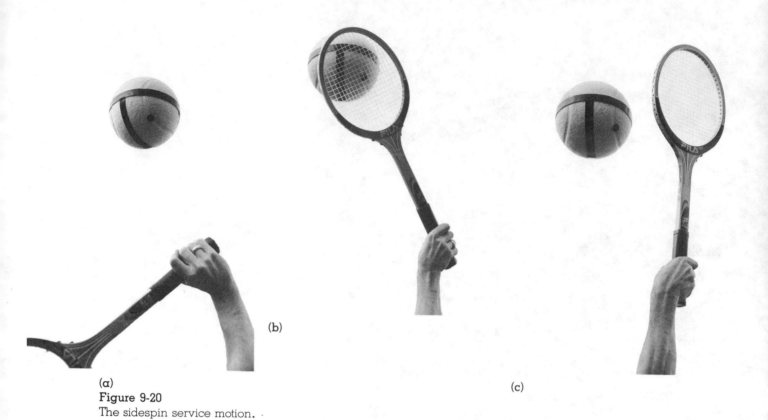

(b)

(a)

(c)

Figure 9-20
The sidespin service motion. ·

and after the "contact sanding period." This looseness will give you a feeling of being totally out of control—so don't panic. Stay with this feeling of giving up control. Ultimately, your best control will be born out of this looseness.

TYPES OF SPIN SERVES

There are two basic types of spin serves that you should concern yourself with. One is sidespin and the other is topspin.

Sidespin

To help you visualize how the ball spins for a sidespin serve, imagine that the ball is the Earth, spinning like a top from west to east. (See Diagram 9–1.)

   To create this spin, toss the ball a little more to your right. The strings must contact the ball

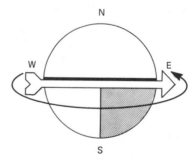

Diagram 9-1
To visualize sidespin, picture the ball as the Earth, spinning from west to east.

somewhere in the lower right hand shaded quadrant (SE). All acceptable "contact sanding options" are *on* or *below* the equator of the ball. The spinning ball should *feel* as if it is traveling *directly up* after it has been sanded.

   The sidespin service motion is very similar to the flat service motion until the beginning of

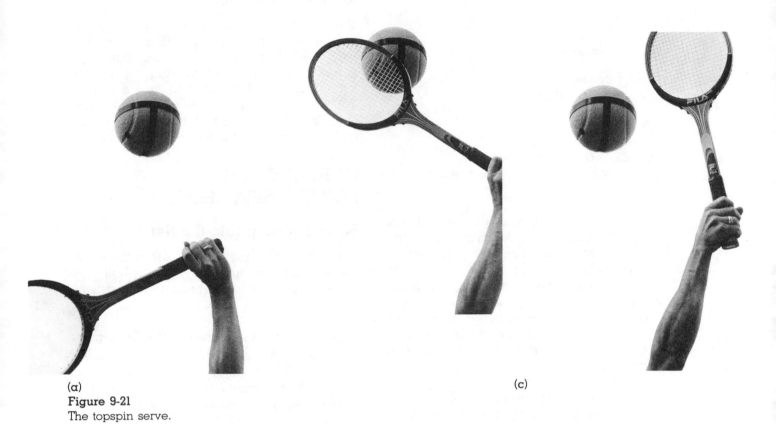

(a)   (c)

Figure 9-21
The topspin serve.

the Raising the Strings Section. At that time, the following occurs:

As the racket is raised, the butt of the handle points directly *up* and leads the strings for an extended period of time. (See Figure 9–20a.)

When the strings finally do get higher than the handle, the strings travel up in the air and in line with the right net post.

"Contact sanding" occurs on the lower right quadrant of the ball, beneath the equator. (See Figure 9–20b.)

The "sanding time" between the ball and strings should be prolonged.

The strings continue to move up and in line with the right net post before, during and just after contact with the ball. (See Figure 9-20c.)

The racket and body complete the sidespin

serve in approximately the same position as in the flat serve.

Placing the Toss for the Sidespin Serve

The toss for a sidespin serve is a little different than the toss for a flat serve. If a correctly tossed ball were permitted to fall, it would land farther to your right than it would for a flat serve. (Refer to the toss for the flat serve in Figure 9–18.)

Topspin

To help you visualize how the ball spins for a topspin serve, picture that the ball is the Earth, rotating forward from southwest to northeast. (See Diagram 9–2.)

To create this spin, the strings must contact the ball somewhere in the lower left-hand shaded quadrant (SW). All acceptable "contact

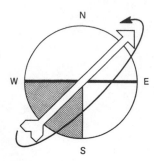

Diagram 9-2
To visualize topspin, picture the Earth rotating forward from southwest to northeast.

sanding options" are *on* or *below* the equator of the ball. The ball should *feel* as if it is traveling *directly up*, after it has been sanded.

Due to the high arc of the ball and its forward rotation, when it lands on your opponent's side it bounces high in the air.

The topspin service motion is very similar to the flat service motion until the beginning of the raising the strings section. At that time, the following occurs:

As the racket is raised, the butt of the handle points directly *up* and leads the strings for an extended period of time. (See Figure 9–21a.)

Before, during and just after contact, the strings should *feel* as though they were first traveling in a *pure vertical path*. This vertical "linear" section will help produce the forward topspin rotation of the ball.

"Contact sanding" occurs on the lower left quadrant of the ball, beneath the equator. (See Figures 9–21b and c.)

The "sanding time" between the ball and strings should be prolonged.

Once the vertical path is completed the strings should travel toward the right side fence. As the racket moves toward the side fence, it should *feel* as though the palm and strings are traveling in a parallel path to the baseline, service line and net.

The racket completes the topspin serve on the left side of the body in approximately the same position as in the flat and sidespin serve.

Placing the Toss for the Topspin Serve

The toss for a topspin serve is a little different from the toss for a flat (hammering) serve. (See Figure 9–22.) If a correctly tossed ball were permitted to fall, it would land somewhere within this round target area, just a little in front of the body and in line with your left toe. Note: If you have a bad back, never toss the ball over your left shoulder or behind you.

CORRECTIONS FOR THE SPIN SERVE

Serve Is Going into the Net

The following corrections contain actions that will enable the strings to program the ball to fly up and over the net. Try one "corrective action" at a time.

Sand further *under* the equator. The strings should feel like they were sanding the South Pole of the ball.

Toss the ball a little closer to your body. This will help you to sand under the equator of the ball.

Toss and contact the ball a little higher up in the air.

Leave the tossing hand up in the air for a longer period of time after the ball leaves the hand. This will keep the left shoulder raised higher than the right, helping the racket to contact the ball under the equator.

Let the butt of the handle lead the strings for an extended period of time as the racket travels up to sand the ball. This action will also help the racket to contact the ball under the equator.

Imagine that the net is *three times* as *high* as it really is. This will encourage you to sand under the equator.

Serve Is Going Long (Past the Service Box)

Create more friction between the strings and the ball.

Minimize the feeling that the strings are

"hammering" the rubber of the ball. Maximize the feeling that the strings are "sanding the cloth" off the ball.

Prolong the sensation of sanding the ball.

Produce more spin by moving your grip in a counterclockwise direction. (Your hand moves closer to the Eastern Backhand Grip. See Grip chapter for further information.) If you begin to slice the ball too much, you might have overdone the grip change.

WHICH SERVE, FLAT OR SPIN, IS MORE IMPORTANT?

Every server gets two opportunities to begin a point. If he is unsuccessful on his second serve, he loses the point. The second serve must therefore be even more reliable than the first. For the following reasons a spin serve is more dependable and should therefore be used for the second serve.

> The spin serve resembles an arc and will be more likely to clear the net by several feet.

> The spin creates a "heavy" tennis ball that will crash to earth soon after it flies over the net, landing in the designated diagonal service box. The high clearance of the net and the crashing effect of the ball are very reliable serving qualities.

For an advanced player, therefore, the spin serve is the more important serve to master. But if you do not have a spin serve, do not panic. Just make sure that your regular serve becomes very reliable. A reliable well-placed second serve—regardless of whether it has spin or not—is what's important.

DEVELOP A RELIABLE FIRST SERVE

While your first serve does not have to be successful 100 percent of the time, it should be successful at least 51 percent of the time.[1] (In

1. The main reason John McEnroe beat Bjorn Borg at Wimbeldon in 1981 is that McEnroe successfully served 104 of 167 first serves.

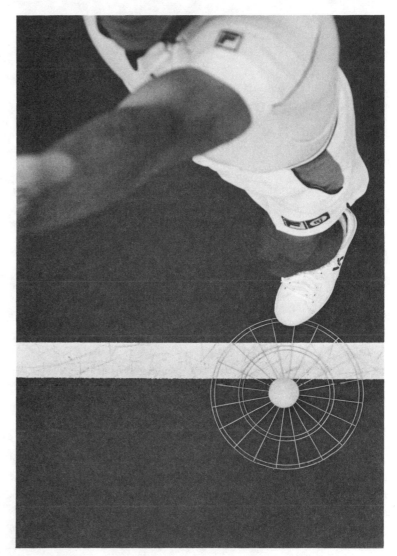

Figure 9-22
The toss for the topspin serve.

doubles it should be successful most of the time.) The more often your first serve goes in, the more pressure your opponent is under. On the other hand, the less often your first serve goes in, the more pressure you are under. Pressure (real or imagined) leads to tension that invariably diminishes the pleasure and precision of your strokes.

If your first serves are not successful *at least* every other time, slow them down. A ball that consistently flies 100 miles per hour into the net helps your opponent and the net repair man, but it doesn't help you. I am not suggesting that you slow your first serve down to five miles an hour, but if it is inconsistent, slow it down a little. A slower, more consistent serve to your opponent's weaker side can be more effective than a fast serve to his stronger side.

HOW TO PRACTICE THE SERVE

Most players use *too much power* when practicing their serves. If power and tension can be eliminated (or at least reduced) during serving practice sessions, then the body will be much more able to "absorb" and understand the correct service motion. When practicing either type of serve, do the following:

Try to serve in slow motion. You might have to toss the ball a little higher to compensate for the slower arm and racket motion. Prolong the gentle contact between the ball and the strings for as long as possible.

Make sure your racket is in constant motion as it is lowered and raised.

Try to keep the feet stationary throughout the entire service motion.

Imagine that a three year old is receiving your serve. The service motion should be gentle enough so as not to injure the child.

Make sure that the shoulder, arm, and wrist remain free, loose, and natural throughout the entire slow-motion serve. Do not use tension to slow the service motion down.

At moment of contact, power should come from just the weight and momentum of the racket; the racket coasts into contact with the ball. At moment of contact, it should feel as if the *racket were serving for you*.

See how much pleasure your body can get from the production of each motion.

Before you add any more power to the serve, be sure that you can serve at least fifteen balls in a row over the net and into the correct service box.

Practice the serve at least once a week. Find a friend who also likes to practice. Even if it's just for the first five minutes of a one hour session, *practice*. Practicing outside of a competitive environment will give you the necessary freedom to experiment with the many imagery actions given in this chapter.

SUMMARY

The strings program the ball on the flat serve to fly over the net and *into* the correct service box.

The strings program the ball on the spin serve (by sanding) to fly *up*, over the net and *into* the correct service box.

Just before contact, the *handle leads the strings*, permitting the strings to touch either *on* or *under the equator of the ball*.

At moment of contact, the wrist is loose and flexible like a hinge. The fingers do *not* squeeze the handle.

To tap the *power* potential of your serve, you must allow the strings to be lowered behind you. Power comes from a *loose pleasurable shoulder* and the *momentum of the racket*, not from a tense wrist.

Pleasure helps create *power and control*. A relaxed body helps make power and control possible.

· *Precision, consistency and placement* are more important than power.

Being *well balanced* and *stationary* will improve the *consistency* of the serve.

chapter
10

The Return
of the Serve

The stroke used to return a ball that has been served is appropriately called the return of serve. Unfortunately, while the server always gets two chances to begin each point, the player receiving the serve only gets one chance to return each successful serve. Therefore, to compete effectively against an opponent with a powerful, consistent, and well-placed serve, you must develop an effective and consistent service return.

The return of serve is a cross between a ground stroke and a volley. It is most similar to a ground stroke in that the ball is contacted after it bounces. It is most similar to a volley in that when returning a fast serve (because time is of the essence and power unnecessary), some of the backswing should be eliminated.

The reason that the serve and return of serve are considered so important is that at advanced levels of tennis, the eventual outcome of a point is often determined by these two strokes. To break your opponent's serve (win a game when he is serving), your return should either neutralize his most offensive stroke or place him on the defensive. Unless your opponent's serve is very weak, do not try to win the point outright.

Remember, you will never be able to beat your opponent if he always wins his serve.

RETURN OF SERVICE STROKE: TWO MOST IMPORTANT ELEMENTS

Two major factors make the return of serve a difficult stroke to produce: the speed of the ball and tension in the body.

Shorten the Backswing

To compensate for the speed of the served ball, prepare the racket early by minimizing the backswing. *By the time the served ball bounces in your service box, the backswing should already be complete.* Go for proper contact, not power. *Use* the power of your opponent's serve. If your opponent's serve is extremely fast, do the above actions and step back from the baseline several feet. (This will give you a little more time to prepare.) Don't stand too far back, however, because angular serves will now be too far away for you to reach in time.

Keep the Body Free of Tension

You should be free of tension as your opponent contacts the ball, as his serve bounces in your service box, and when you contact the ball. Many players, however, have tension in their body during at least one of the above three times. The entire return of service stroke should be a pleasurable and nurturing experience. Try to *embrace the serve, not brace for it.* Your body should be open, focused, and relaxed at moment of contact.

To induce a relaxed state, try to do the following:

1. Gently breathe (in or out) at least during one of the following times:
   a. before your opponent serves,
   b. as your opponent contacts the ball,
   c. as the ball lands in your service box,
   d. as you produce the return of service motion.
2. Watch the ball bounce in your service box. Take a mental picture of the bounce and say "click" as you do so. This imaginary act of taking a picture helps to line the ball up and to alleviate tension.
3. Watch the moment of contact between the ball and your racket. This action will help you to focus your attention on the ball rather than your opponent.
4. Keep your shoulder relaxed and free of tension at moment of contact.
5. Remember that you are contacting just the ball, *not* your opponent. The ball is not alive; it is only composed of rubber and cloth.

STROKE PRODUCTION SUGGESTIONS

Forehand

1. Visualize the energy, direction, and control of your return of serve coming from your palm rather than the strings.
2. Create a linear section.
3. Try to prolong the moment of contact.

Backhand

1. Imagine that the energy, direction, and control of your stroke is coming from your knuckles (especially the pinky knuckle).
2. Get the feeling that the handle butt is leading the strings throughout the entire forward path of the racket.
3. Create the stroke without any wrist movement.
4. Create a linear section.
5. Try to prolong the moment of contact.

Two-Handed Backhand

1. Visualize the energy, direction, and control of your stroke as coming from your left palm.
2. Create a linear section.
3. Try to prolong the moment of contact.

WHERE TO WAIT FOR THE SERVE

A competent server has the potential to serve the ball either to your forehand or to your backhand. So, while waiting for the ball, you

Diagram 10-1

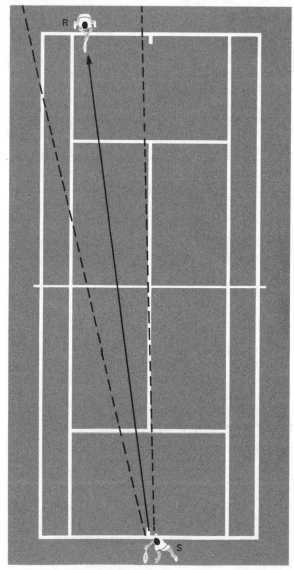

Diagram 10-2

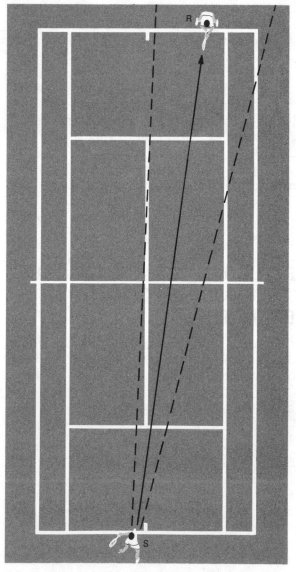

Stand halfway between your opponent's potential service angle.

Figure 10-1
Receiving in your right service box (the deuce service box).

should stand halfway between his potential forehand and backhand service angle (see Diagrams 10–1 and 2.

Receiving in Your Right Service Box (The Deuce Service Box)

Assuming your opponent is a right-handed server, prepare to receive his serve by standing just behind the baseline with your right foot in line with the right singles sideline (see Figure 10–1). You are now favoring your right side because a right-handed server's ball usually moves to *your* right after it bounces. This is especially true for most types of spin serves.

If your opponent is a left-handed server, move two to three feet to the left of the singles sideline. You should be in this position because a left-handed spin serve tends to move to *your* left after it bounces.

Receiving in Your Left Service Box (The Advantage Service Box)

Assuming your opponent is a right-handed server, prepare to receive his serve by standing just behind the baseline with your left shoe two to three feet away from the left singles sideline. You should favor your right side because the serve tends to move to *your* right after it bounces. (See Figure 10–2.)

If your opponent is a left-handed server, move two to three feet to the left. Your left shoe is now in line with the left singles sideline. You should be in this position because a left-handed server's ball tends to move to *your* left after it bounces.

Use the above positioning when you are unfamiliar with your opponent's serve. As soon as you detect a pattern, however, change your position to adjust to his serve.

Figure 10-2
Receiving in your left service box (the advantage service box).

If your opponent "dinks" his serve over and in (especially his second serve), wait for his return several feet inside the baseline.

If your opponent always angles his serves, favor the angular side. He might be incapable of serving non-angular serves.

If your opponent's serve is very fast, you might want to wait for it several feet behind the baseline.

PLACEMENT OF THE RETURN OF SERVE

Assuming your opponent has an efficient offensive serve, your main goal should be to neutralize it, so that both of you now have an equal chance of winning the point. (Example: If someone approached you with a knife [offense] your first goal would *not* be to punch him in the nose [offense]. You would first want to disarm him so that you both start off even [neutral].)

Unless you are an advanced or tournament player, your goal should never be to win the point outright with your return of serve. Go for placement, not power.

Your placement of the return of serve will depend on whether your opponent runs up to net or not, after serving.

Server Runs Up to Net

When your opponent runs up to the net after serving, it is because he intends to volley the ball. (See Diagram 10–3.) If he can contact the ball at a height above the net, his volley will usually be an offensive one. For this reason, your return should be *low over the net* (assuming you are not going to lob), which will cause the ball to land shallow in his court (near the service line). If he is able to reach the ball he will be forced to volley it at a height below the net, causing a defensive return. If he is not able to volley it, and it bounces at his feet, he will have to use a ground stroke called the half-volley, which is also a very difficult stroke to produce.

The more relaxed and comfortable you can become when your opponent approaches the net, the more sophisticated your low return of service strokes can become. You should eventually have the ability to:

return the ball to his weaker volleying side;

gently send the ball past him; or

direct the ball at his feet.

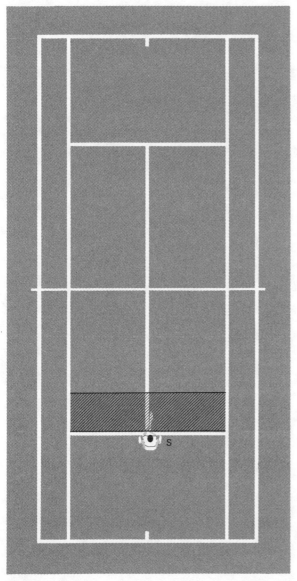

Diagram 10 3
When your opponent runs up to the net, return the ball low over the net.

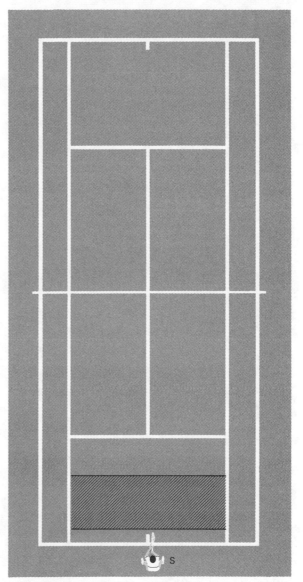

Diagram 10 4
When your opponent stays back, return the ball with greater net clearance.

Remember that all of these shots must fly *low* over the net and land shallow in his court.

Server Stays Back After Serving

When your opponent stays back after serving, your goal is to force him to remain behind the baseline when contacting your return. (See Diagram 10–4.) To accomplish this, the ball should clear the net by several feet and land deep in your opponent's court. This type of service return will usually neutralize his serve. For example, a deep return to your opponent's backhand side (weaker side) can be a very

effective shot. You can also return a short, excessively angular, cross-court shot, because your opponent will have difficulty reaching it in time.

SUMMARY

Because time is of the essence, shorten the backswing of most return of service strokes.

Power should be the last ingredient that is added to a return of service stroke. Think pleasurable placement, not power.

Spins

After you contact the ball, it has the potential to spin (rotate) in different directions as it flies back over the net. The advantage of spinning a tennis ball is that the spin can help you to consistently send the ball back over the net and *into* the opponent's court. This is because all types of spin make it easier for the ball to consistently land within the confines of your opponent's court. Spins can enable players to experience an enormous amount of feel, touch, control, and finesse. They also give the player the ability to alter dramatically the behavior of the ball once it bounces.

While you can still become a very advanced player without knowing how to spin the ball, learning to produce spin can give you more options that will make tennis a more enjoyable and creative sport.

There are basically two major types of spins to learn: *topspin* and *backspin*. Each spin alters the behavior of the ball in a different way. Attention: In order to help you visualize the concept of topspin and backspin, I have chosen a car tire to represent the ball. Because the tire is so much larger than a tennis ball, my form and the path of the racket had to be consequently altered. Therefore, do not try to copy my exact form. Rather, use the tire image to get the general idea of how to produce these two different types of spins.

TOPSPIN

Imagine that the ball is an automobile tire with a constant horizontal equator. (See Figure 11-1.) Imagine also that the top of the tire is the North Pole and the bottom of the tire is the South Pole. Topspin occurs when the *strings* of the racket *contact* the *equator* of the tire in such a way as to cause the arrows to move *up*, disappearing over the top of the tire. (The arrows appear in the South and disappear in the North.) When the tire is spinning forward in this manner topspin has been created. Many players mistakenly believe that topspin is created by plac-

ing the strings on top of the ball. *Do not try to create topspin by touching the top of the ball.* What you will produce is a ball that goes directly into the net.

Topspin Forehand

Note that the strings begin much lower than the ball (the racket backward section) and at the completion of the stroke they are extremely high in the air (the follow-forward section). (See Figures 11-2a through d.)

Topspin Backhand

Note that the strings once again begin much lower than the ball (the racket backward section) and at the completion of the stroke they are extremely high in the air (the follow-forward section). (See Figures 11-3a through d.)

HOW TO CREATE A TOPSPIN STROKE

Before, during, and after contact the strings should travel in a low to high linear (not circular) vertical ascent. The more you want the "tire" to spin, the lower your racket and hand must be as you begin, and the higher up your racket and hand must be when the stroke is completed. Before contacting the ball the strings can be lowered by:

> Dropping the head (strings) of the racket. The butt of the handle will now be higher than the strings.
>
> Bending from the knees (not from the waist). This bending will automatically lower the racket.

Experiment to see which "lowering" method produces the most successful and consistent topspin.

Some players exaggerate the vertical lift of the racket by first lowering the body (by bending the knees) before contact and by then

Opposite page: Figure 11-1
Topspin occurs when the strings contact the equator
of the tire so as to cause the arrows to move up over the top of the tire.

Figure 11-2
The topspin forehand.

(a)

(b)

Figure 11-3
The topspin backhand.

(a)

(b)

(c)

(d)

(c)

(d)

raising the body by extending their bent legs as they contact the ball. If you want to experiment with this "bending and extending" action be sure not to overexaggerate the extending movement of the body. Too much upward body movement jeopardizes the precision of the stroke.

Topspin Forehand

The *palm* is the focal point for direction and power. Be sure the palm creates a low to high follow-forward stroke rather than a low to high circular follow-through. There must be minimal wrist action in order to consistently produce a *low to high linear vertical section.*

Topspin Backhand (One-Handed)

The *pinky knuckle* is the focal point for direction and power. Be sure the pinky creates a low to high follow-forward stroke rather than a low to high circular follow-through. When the stroke is completed it should *feel* as if the pinky knuckle had been leading the strings. *Eliminate all wrist action* in order to consistently produce a *low to high linear vertical section.*

Topspin Backhand (Two-Handed)

The *left palm* (for right-handed players) is the focal point for direction and power. Be sure the left palm creates a low to high follow-forward, rather than a low to high circular follow-through. Once again, there must be minimal wrist action in order to consistently produce a *low to high linear vertical section.*

Sand the Equator Off the Ball

A tennis ball is composed of two substances: rubber and cloth. To create topspin it is most helpful to focus most of your attention on the cloth rather than on the rubber of the ball. Imagine the strings are sandpaper and the stationary equator of the ball is composed of cloth. Your objective is to "throw" your hand up, which will in turn cause the strings to sand or de-fuzz the cloth off the equator of the ball.[1] Topspin is the result of friction that is created

between the ball and strings as you produce the *vertical linear contact section.* (See Diagram 11–1.)

As you can see in Figure 11–4a, the strings begin much lower than the ball. Sand on the equator with a flat or slightly closed racket face. The strings should feel as though they are traveling directly *up.* The strings complete the stroke very high in the air. (See Figure 11–4b.)

Try to imagine that you are *sanding* the *ball straight up* (like the path of a rocket ship). Do not be afraid to exaggerate the "straight up" motion of the hand and strings. In reality the ball will not travel straight up, and the vertical linear path of your hand and racket won't be straight up, but your "straight up sanding attempt" is what is important.

To experience more control, touch, and feel, *try* to prolong the time that the strings are "sanding" the ball. This can be accomplished by elongating the linear contact section of the stroke.

Some players prefer to produce a topspin forehand by slightly closing the face of the racket (down face). This down face racket is usually caused by a Semi-Western Grip. (See Grip chapter for details.) Its advantage is that it creates more spin on the ball.

To successfully produce topspin by using a closed face, do two things:

Diagram 11-1
Path of the racket before, during, and after contact as it creates topspin.

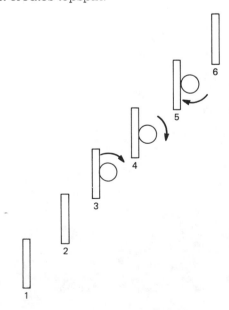

---

1. For backspin (next section) your objective is to sand or de-fuzz the cloth *under* the equator of the ball.

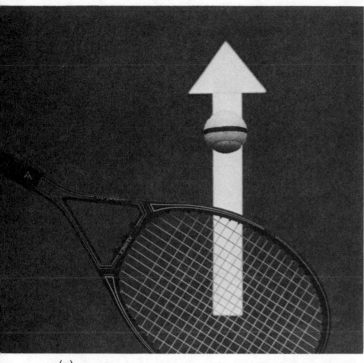

(a)
Figure 11-4

1. Try to sand *under the equator*. Obviously, it is impossible to point the face of the racket down and sand the ball under the equator, but this exaggerated image will help you to sand the ball *on* the *equator* rather than incorrectly on top of the equator.

2. Exaggerate the vertical low to high path of the racket. The linear path of the racket now must be more vertical and less horizontal than usual. You can lower the strings by bending your knees more.

Characteristics of a Topspin Ball

The forward spin of the ball causes it to react in the following manner:

Once it clears the net, the ball will crash to earth. (See Diagram 11–2.)

The greater the spin, the more pronounced the downward crashing arc.

Topspin creates a *high bouncing ball*. Because of this energized bounce, the ball will travel a further distance (in feet) once it lands.

When a topspin ball bounces, it *appears* to increase in speed and power.

Advantages of a Topspin Ball

Because of its crashing effect, the ball can clear the net by many feet and not fly out of bounds. A player is doing well when he strokes a ball powerfully and it clears the

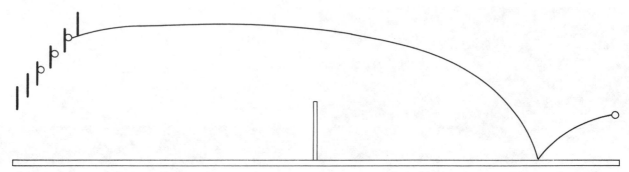

Diagram 11-2
The path of a ball with topspin.

net by five to ten feet, and yet it still lands inside the baseline by several feet. Only topspin can offer these options.

You are free to use a good deal of pleasurable power (not tension) when creating topspin. You can channel much linear and vertical energy into this stroke without causing the ball to fly past the baseline.

Because the laws of physics will take care of the ball landing within the confines of your opponent's court, your main concern is to have the ball clear the net. If you can *sand* the ball *up*, the spin of the ball will do the rest.

Because of the energized bounce of the ball, your opponent usually will be forced to wait for the ball while standing behind the baseline. If you can keep your opponent far behind the baseline, then certain shots (side angular shots, drop shots, drop volleys, etc.) will be extremely effective. (See Specialty Shot Chapter for detailed information.)

Your short cross-court angular shots (landing near or in the service box) become more successful due to the crashing effect of the ball. The ball will land immediately after it clears the net, rather than possibly floating out of bounds (wide).

When your opponent is playing the net, a low topspin shot (low net clearance) will force him to volley the ball below the height of the net, due to the crashing effect of the ball. Contacting the ball at this height usually causes him to produce a defensive volley.

Disadvantages of a Topspin Ball

It is difficult to produce topspin consistently, especially on the backhand side.

The stroke is also difficult to produce when you are in an uncomfortable or unstable position, such as when you are running for the ball; or you are off balance (usually with your weight falling backwards); or you are contacting a ball that is lower than your knees or higher than your shoulders; or your opponent's ball is approaching at a fast speed; or the ball is coming directly at you.

BACKSPIN

Imagine once again that the ball is a tire with a constant horizontal equator. Imagine also that the top of the tire is the North Pole and the bottom of the tire is the South Pole. Backspin occurs when the *strings* of the racket contact *under* the *equator* of the tire in such a way as to cause the arrows to move *down*, disappearing under the bottom of the tire. (The arrows appear in the North and disappear in the South.) (See Figure 11–5.) When the tire is spinning in this manner, backspin has been created. To create more backspin, the strings must *sand further under the equator* of the ball.

How to Create a Backspin Stroke

Backspin, like topspin, is produced by creating friction between the strings and ball. The friction, however, is now created *under* the equator by sanding or de-fuzzing the cloth (not the rubber) off the ball.

When the racket is brought back, the strings can be either flat or semi-open faced. During the racket forward and the linear contact section, however, the strings should always remain or be placed in a semi-open faced position. This will allow you to sand way *underneath* the equator of the ball. (See Figures 11-6a through c and 11-7a through c.) Unlike other strokes that begin low and end high, the backspin arm and racket motion is more horizontal and less vertical. (See Diagram 11-3.) Because the ball tends to follow the forward path of the hand and racket, the hand and strings should be a little higher than the net at the completion of this gradual low to high linear contact section.

If you produce backspin with the hand and racket traveling from a high to a very low position (a descending linear contact path), your shot will probably fly into the net or be a defensive shot. This high to low swing is usually referred to as a "chopping" or "hacking" motion. Unless you are a very gifted athlete, you should avoid a high to low stroke.

Always try to prolong the "sanding time" between the ball and strings. If you find that your ball doesn't have enough spin, sand closer to the South Pole of the ball. If you find that your backspin ball has too much spin, or flies too high in the air, sand closer to the equator.

In order for you to consistently produce a linear section, there must be minimal wrist action. The focal point for backspin should therefore be the *hand* rather than the wrist. The hand will encourage you to create linear strokes while the wrist will incorrectly produce circular strokes.

Note: In the following forehand and backhand pictures, the only reason that the forward path of the racket is not horizontal is due to the large size of the tire.

Forehand

The *palm* is the focal point for direction and power. Be sure to elongate the linear contact section.

Backhand (One-Handed)

The *pinky knuckle* is the focal point for direction and power. Be sure to exaggerate the linear contact section. When the stroke is completed it

Figure 11-5
Backspin
The arrows appear in the North and disappear in the South.

should *feel* as if the pinky knuckle is leading the strings. This can be done by eliminating all wrist action.

Backhand (Two-Handed)

The *left palm* (for a right-handed player) is the focal point for direction and power. Be sure the left palm elongates the linear contact section.

Characteristics of a Backspin Ball

The forward flight and backward spin of the ball causes it to react in the following manner:

(a)　　　　　　　(b)　　　　　　　(c)

Figure 11-6
The backspin forehand.

Once the ball clears the net it will tend to float more than topspin. It will not rapidly crash like topspin. (See Diagram 11-4.)

Once it lands, an offensive backspin ball tends to create a lower bouncing ball than topspin.

A backspin ball with low net clearance will stay low after it bounces.

Advantages of Backspin

You do not need a full backswing or follow-forward to produce backspin. The path of the racket need not be long or sophisticated. The main ingredient of a backspin stroke is simply to have the strings touch underneath the equator as the racket travels forward.

Because a backspin stroke is more of a horizontal linear path and less of an ascending vertical linear path (topspin) you are *less* likely to mis-hit the ball.

Backspin is easier to produce than topspin if you are in an unstable position, such as when you have little time to prepare for the approaching ball; or the ball is approaching you at a fast speed; or the ball is coming directly at you; or you are off balance (usually with your weight falling backward); or you are in motion (running) at moment of contact.

This spin is easier to produce (than topspin) when you must contact the ball at a height that is not "ideal," such as when it is below the knees or above the shoulders.

It is slightly easier to get the feeling of prolonging the "sanding time" between the strings and the ball when using backspin. The moment of contact tends to give one a *feeling* of having a little more control.

A ball that is gently sanded by your strings (under the equator) will tend to "stop" or "die" after it lands. This is the only spin that

(a)   (b)   (c)

Figure 11-7
The backspin backhand.

Diagram 11-3
Path of the racket before,
during, and after contact.

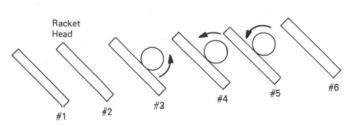

Diagram 11-4
The path of the ball.

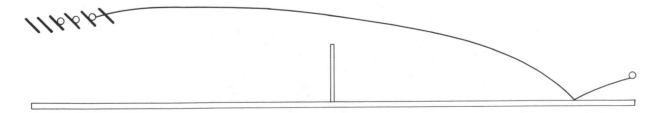

can be used effectively for producing such versatile strokes as drop shots, drop or stop volleys, and short gentle angular shots (see Specialty Shots Chapter).

Because the ball tends to float more than with topspin (it has more of a horizontal descent), you can now get it to land deeper in your opponent's court.

Backspin is an easier and more dependable spin to use when volleying the ball.

Disadvantages of Backspin

Because a backspin ball tends to float more than a topspin ball, it is harder to add power to the ball and still have it land within your opponent's court.

Producing this spin can promote tension in the shoulder and the arm because many players incorrectly use a pushing, punching, chopping, or jabbing motion to achieve backspin.

Many players create this motion improperly by causing the hand and racket to travel in a high to low motion. The ball will then either fly into the net or land shallow on your opponent's side of the court, creating a defensive shot.

It is hard to create offensive ground strokes (forehand and backhand) because the ball tends to float.

Extreme cross-court angular shots become difficult to produce because the ball tends to float wide and land outside of your opponent's court.

Your opponent is more likely to produce an offensive return when volleying your backspin ball because your ball floats (remains higher than the net) rather than crashes once it clears the net.

When the wind is at your back (with you), the ball will tend to float more and can land outside of your opponent's court.

SUMMARY

Topspin is created when the strings of the racket contact the equator of the ball in such a way as to cause the arrows to move up, disappearing over the *top* of the ball. The strings must *feel* like they are traveling in almost a pure vertical path (linear contact section) to successfully and consistently produce this spin.

Backspin is created when the strings contact *under* the *equator* of the ball in such a way as to cause the arrows to move down, disappearing under the bottom of the ball. The strings should travel in a gradual low to high horizontal path (linear contact section) to successfully and consistently produce this spin.

chapter
12

The Specialty Shots

We have already discussed the four fundamental strokes in tennis: the forehand, backhand, serve, and volley. By using these four fundamental strokes as building blocks, we can also create other strokes. I call these strokes specialty shots. They are produced by slightly altering the fundamental strokes. Specialty shots are usually used for specific purposes and can be very effective tools when properly executed. The specialty shots that will be discussed in this chapter are:

Drop Shot   Lob
Drop Volley   Overhead Smash
Passing Shot   Approach Shot

The drop shot and drop volley are grouped together because they are both gentle finesse shots. The drop shot is produced after the ball bounces, while the drop volley is produced on a fly.

THE DROP SHOT

Characteristics

The ball travels at a slow speed over the net.

The ball has an abundance of backspin.

The ball clears the net by a safe margin (at least one to two feet). As the ball leaves your strings, its ascent should be slightly vertical.

Once the ball clears the net its descent follows a *vertical path*, allowing it to land close to your opponent's side of the net. (See Diagram 12–1.)

Once it bounces, the ball's motion is vertical, not forward.

Purposes

To win the point outright.

To cause your opponent to run up to the net and to contact the ball below the height of

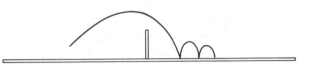

Diagram 12-1
The path of the ball during the drop shot.

the net, which will usually produce a defensive return.

To force your opponent to come to net so that you can lob your next shot over his head, or force him to volley (assuming he has a weak volley).

To tire your opponent by causing him to run.

To catch your opponent off guard, by surprising him.

When to Produce a Drop Shot

When you are standing inside the baseline. The closer you are to the net, the easier and more successful this stroke will be.

When your opponent's shot is slow or medium paced.

When Not to Produce a Drop Shot

When you are standing behind the baseline.

When a strong wind is behind the ball (A strong wind will give the ball too much forward momentum and it will reach your opponent too soon).

When your opponent hits a fast powerful shot. (It will be hard to slow his ball down in order to produce this slow finesse shot.)

When your opponent is standing near the net.

How to Produce an Effective Drop Shot

1. Racket Backward Section. Your racket preparation should disguise the fact that

Opposite page: Figure 12-1
Sand the cloth off the ball at the South Pole.

you are about to produce a drop shot. Your racket preparation should therefore be similar to your regular forehand and backhand ground stroke preparation.

2. Linear Contact and Follow-Forward Sections.

  a. Your racket and hand travel forward on a *horizontal* plane just before, during, and after contact. It is risky to produce a drop shot by moving your racket and hand from a high to a low position (a downward chopping motion), because the ball will tend to follow the downward path of the racket and hand and fly into the net.

  b. *Just* before, during, and after contact, your racket travels at a slower speed, with an open racket face.

  c. The strings contact the ball way underneath the equator. Imagine the strings as sandpaper. Try to "sand" the cloth off the ball at the South Pole (If your sanding attempt produces a ball with too much forward momentum (speed) and not enough spin, sand further under the equator of the ball. See Figure 12–1.)

THE DROP VOLLEY

Characteristics

The characteristics of the drop volley are similar to those of the drop shot. (Review Drop Shot Section and see Diagram 12–2.)

Purposes

The main purpose of the drop volley is to win the point outright.

When to Produce a Drop Volley

When you are standing inside the service line. The closer you are to the net the easier this shot becomes.

When your opponent's shot is slow or medium-paced.

When your opponent is standing behind the baseline.

When Not to Produce the Drop Volley

When you are standing behind the service line.

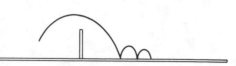

Diagram 12-2
The path of the ball during the drop volley.

When you are volleying a hard-hit ball.

When you are contacting the ball at a height above the shoulders. (It is difficult to physically produce a drop volley from this height.)

When your opponent is standing inside the baseline.

How to Produce a Drop Volley

All backswing should be eliminated from your racket preparation.

Contact with the ball occurs in front of the body.

Just before, during, and after contact there is very little forward arm and racket movement.

The strings contact way underneath the equator of the ball with an open racket face. This will produce backspin.

At moment of contact, your hand and the strings of the racket should feel as if they had fully *absorbed* the tennis ball. Like a sponge, the strings absorb the momentum and power of the ball. (See Figure 12–2.)

At moment of contact with the ball the fingers should be fairly relaxed.

Your hand and racket at moment of contact must develop a feeling of gentle control.

THE PASSING SHOT

The passing shot is executed when your opponent is playing the net. A successful shot sends the ball past him either on his left or right side.

Characteristics

Effective passing shots fly *low* over the net. This assumes that even if your opponent reaches the ball in time to contact it, his return will usually be defensive. This is because he will have to volley it at a height lower than the net. Therefore, most passing shots should be thought of as *low-over-the-net-and-in-shots.*

A passing shot need not be fast, powerful, or aggressive, so long as it is out of your opponent's reach. A passing shot can be gentle as long as it is low and well placed.

A passing shot with topspin (see Topspin Section) creates the most effective passing shot. Topspin helps the ball to crash to earth once it clears the net. This crashing effect helps to make your opponent volley the ball below the height of the net.

Purposes

To send the ball past your opponent (when he is playing the net).

To force him to contact the ball at a height lower than the net, just in case your shot does not pass him.

When to Produce a Passing Shot

When your opponent is at the net and you are able to produce an offensive or neutral shot.

You can produce a passing shot from any position on the court. They become less effective, however, the farther back you are from the baseline. This is because your opponent now has more time to prepare for his volley.

When Not to Produce a Passing Shot

When your opponent is waiting *very* close to the net. In such a case lob over his head rather than try a passing shot. Lobs are very effective when your opponent is "crowding the net."

When your passing shot will be defensive because you are in a physically awkward position. In such a case, rather than produce a passing shot, lob the ball over your opponent's head.

When you know your opponent's volley is weak. In such a case send the ball directly at him. If he is right-handed, his most vulnerable area is his right hip. (Reverse the hip if he is a lefty.)

Figure 12-2
The strings absorb the power
and momentum of the ball like a sponge.

How to Produce a Passing Shot

There are two passing shot options open to you. Which one you choose depends upon your skill at placing the ball and upon your opponent's volleying ability.

1. *Down-the-Line Passing Shot:* When producing a down-the-line passing shot (ball travels parallel and close to the doubles alley), remember that the net is higher at the net posts than in the center. Therefore, a down-the-line passing shot must have a slightly higher trajectory.

2. *Excessively Angular Cross-Court Shot:* You can also pass your opponent by using an excessively angular cross-court shot, created by placing your strings more on the side of the ball. Use more finesse and spin and less power when creating this stroke.

Remember, do not try "to hit" the ball past your opponent. Rather "throw" your palm (forehand) or pinky (backhand) past him.

THE LOB

The lob is a high-arcing ball. It is usually used as a neutralizing or a defensive stroke.

Characteristics

The ball travels in a high arc.

The ball bounces high in the air after it lands.

The ball usually has little or no spin, unless it is a topspin lob.

Purposes

When your opponent is at the baseline:

1. To cause your opponent to remain behind the baseline. (This will keep him in a less offensive position.)
2. To throw his timing and rhythm off, especially if he is accustomed to receiving fast tennis balls.
3. To cause him to contact the ball above his head. Many players have difficulty contacting high tennis balls, especially on the backhand side.
4. To annoy or unnerve your opponent.
5. To allow you to stall for time (when you are out of position).
6. To give you extra time to run to net. (While somewhat unorthodox, this action can surprise your opponent, who does not expect you to approach the net after you send up a lob.)

When your opponent is at net:

1. To enable you to win the point outright.
2. To exhaust your opponent by forcing him to run after the ball.
3. To cause your opponent to use his overhead smash (assuming his overhead is weak).

When to Produce a Lob

When you are standing on or behind the baseline.

When there is little or no wind.

When the sun is shining in your opponent's eyes.

When there aren't any clouds (your opponent will have difficulty with his depth perception).

When Not to Produce a Lob

When your lobs are weak and your opponent's overhead smashes are strong.

When your opponent is playing the net and his volleys are very weak. In such a case, make him volley the ball.

When the wind is very strong.

How to Produce an Effective Lob

Your racket preparation for the lob should be similar to your regular forehand and backhand preparation. In other words, your opponent should not be expecting a lob (especially when he is at the net).

Your racket and hand should feel as though they are producing a low to high linear stroke; with the strings touching under the equator of the ball.

It should *feel* as if your racket were *carrying* (not hitting) the ball high over the net.

It should also *feel* as if your hand (either the palm or the pinky) were leaving the body and flying high over the net. Rather than lobbing the ball in the air, get the feeling you are lobbing your palm or pinky in the air.

Your arm and shoulder movement should be gentle, fluid, graceful, and free of tension.

Do not be afraid of lobbing the ball long. Many players lob too short because they are afraid of losing the point long. This fear causes tension in the shoulder and arm, which in turn produces short lobs.

THE OVERHEAD SMASH

The overhead smash and the serve are very similar motions. When you serve, however, you toss the ball to yourself. When you produce an overhead shot your opponent is tossing the ball to you in the form of a high arcing lob.

It is interesting to note that most players never practice the overhead stroke, yet always assume that their overheads should be successful. As with all strokes, the overhead must be practiced separately. If you do not practice and still attempt to smash each overhead, you may find that only some of your attempts will be successful. Before adding power, make sure that you can first produce a gentle, relaxed, and consistent overhead.

Characteristics

The ball is contacted high above the head.

The stroke is an offensive shot.

The stroke can be produced before or after the ball bounces.

Purposes

To win the point outright.

To put your opponent on the defensive.

When to Produce an Overhead Smash

When you are near the net. The closer you are to the net, the easier this stroke usually becomes.

When your opponent produces an ineffective lob that does not fly over your head (when you are playing the net). This is a great set-up for an overhead smash.

When Not to Produce an Overhead Smash

When you are way behind the baseline. The further away from the net you are the more difficult this stroke becomes.

During a strong wind. It is difficult to produce a consistent overhead smash when the wind moves your opponent's lob around.

When the sun is directly in your eyes.

How to Produce an Effective Overhead Smash

Preparation

1. Lining Up the Ball

You must anticipate the entire arc and path of your opponent's ball *before* it

Figure 12-3
For an overhead smash,
make believe you first want to catch the ball.

reaches you. This is one of the most difficult parts of the overhead. To simplify lining up the ball, make believe you want *to catch* your opponent's ball in your left hand rather than hit it with your racket. (See Figure 12–3.) To accomplish this do the following:

a) Immediately turn your left side to the net.

b) At the same time, raise your left arm high above your head (your left palm is toward the sky with the back of your hand facing you). You are now in the *side catching position*. Note: If you need to move back, for speed, safety, and positioning, always move with your side to the net, never run backwards.

2. Preparing the Racket

Prepare the racket at the same time you are getting into the side catching position. The racket should *immediately* be placed in the half service position with the strings lower than the shoulders. However, do not bring the racket down, around, and back, as you would when serving. Instead, to save time, bring the racket up above the head and down the back.

Beginning the Arm Motion

1. As in the serve, the butt of the handle leads the strings as the racket goes up to meet the ball. This action helps the strings to touch either on or under the equator of the ball.

2. The left "catching arm" remains high in the air for an extended period of time. This action will keep the left shoulder higher than the right shoulder. This relationship will encourage the ball to fly over the net (when the racket contacts it). The arm lowers just before the strings contact the ball.

3. You must start the stroke *earlier* with the overhead smash than with the serve, because the *ball* is now *falling faster*. It should feel as if you will probably miss the ball. Go up to contact the ball "too soon" rather than wait for it to come to you.

Moment of Contact

1. As with the serve, at moment of contact, the fingers and wrist should be very loose. Initially, it might feel as though you have lost power and control. In reality, just the opposite is the case: you gain power and control. At moment of contact make sure you are not squeezing the fingers too tightly.[1] Gain control through pleasure and freedom rather than tension and power. At moment of contact, the power should *feel* as if it were just coming from the weight and momentum of the racket.

2. Regardless of how powerful your stroke is, always try to prolong the moment of contact between the ball and strings.

[1]. By lowering the right hand so that the pinky is off the handle—now only four fingers are holding the racket—you can automatically create a loose wrist.

3. Do *not* rush to lower the racket arm too quickly after contact, as your strings will tend to contact the ball too much above the equator.

Follow-Through

1. The right shoulder and arm should be loose and relaxed. The motion should be a soothing pleasurable one, not aggressive and tense.

2. The right arm and racket should lower and cross over the body at the completion of the stroke.

3. At the completion of the stroke, the body should be balanced and stationary.

THE APPROACH SHOT

The ground stroke that is produced so that you can run up to the net to volley is called the approach shot. An effective approach shot will prevent your opponent from producing an offensive return.

Characteristics

The characteristics of an approach shot are not as specific as for most other specialty shots. Your approach shot will usually be successful as long as it places your opponent in a weak, non-offensive, and/or off balance position when he contacts the ball.

Purpose

The approach shot allows you to safely approach the net with enough time to prepare to volley.

When to Produce an Approach Shot

When you are standing at least five feet inside the baseline. The closer you are to the net when producing your approach shot, the easier it will be for you to run into the correct volley position so that you can be prepared to volley. The correct volley position is approximately ten feet away from the net. In the Doubles Chapter this area is referred to as the second channel, or the offensive volley position. Your goal after executing an approach shot is to arrive into this channel with enough time to prepare to volley. Remember that while your goal is to enter the second (offensive)

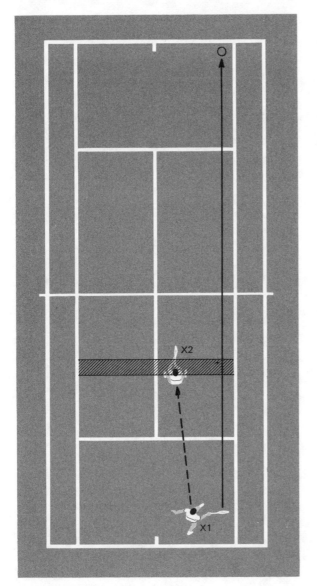

Diagram 12-3

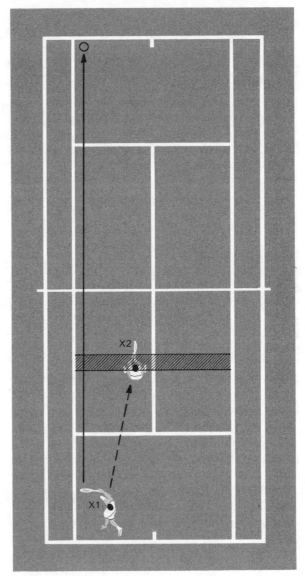

Diagram 12-4

X_1 = Your position for the approach shot. O = Where your approach shot lands.
X_2 = Where you run in (the channel) to await your opponent's passing shot.

channel (see Diagrams 12–3 through 12–6), an even more important goal is to *stop* (regardless of your court position) just *before* your opponent contacts the ball. This is because it is very difficult to volley from a running position.

When Not to Produce an Approach Shot

Regardless of how powerful and offensive your approach shot is, do *not* approach the net when contacting the ball on or behind the baseline. Starting from on or behind the baseline will *not* give you enough time to run into the channel and be prepared to volley. Wait for a better opportunity.

How to Produce an Approach Shot

Your regular forehand and backhand ground strokes should be used when producing an approach shot. It is advisable, however, to be in a stationary position while making this shot unless you are an advanced player. A successful approach shot should place your opponent in a weak, vulnerable, and/or off-balance position when he contacts the ball. Following is a list of acceptable approach shots:

1. Produce a shot that forces your opponent to attempt his passing shot while standing outside of the boundaries of the singles court.

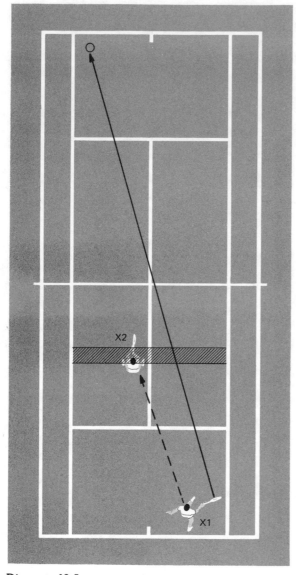

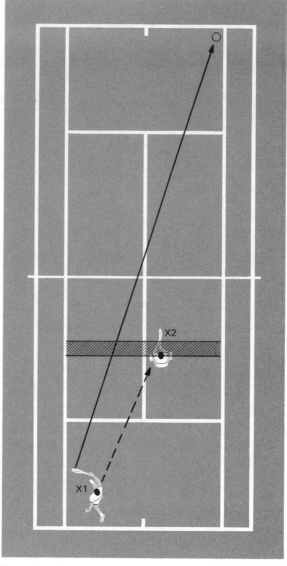

Diagram 12-5   **Diagram 12-6**

X_1 = Your position for the approach shot. O = Where your approach shot lands.
X_2 = Where you run in (the channel) to await your opponent's passing shot.

2. Direct your approach shot to your opponent's weaker side (usually his backhand).

3. Force your opponent to be in motion while contacting the ball.

4. Force your opponent to contact the ball at one of two heights:

   a. *Above His Head*.
      Unless your opponent is a tournament player he will probably not be able to make an offensive return when he contacts the ball above his head, especially on his weaker side.

   b. *Below the Height of the Net*.
      It is very difficult for your opponent to produce an offensive return when he is forced to contact the ball below the height of the net. Most tournament players therefore produce low flying backspin approach shots because this type of shot usually stays low after it bounces.

Notice that X needs to run a shorter distance into the channel when he produces a down-the-line shot (see Diagrams 12–3 and 12–4) than when he produces a cross-court shot (see Diagrams 12–5 and 12–6).

chapter
13

The Grips

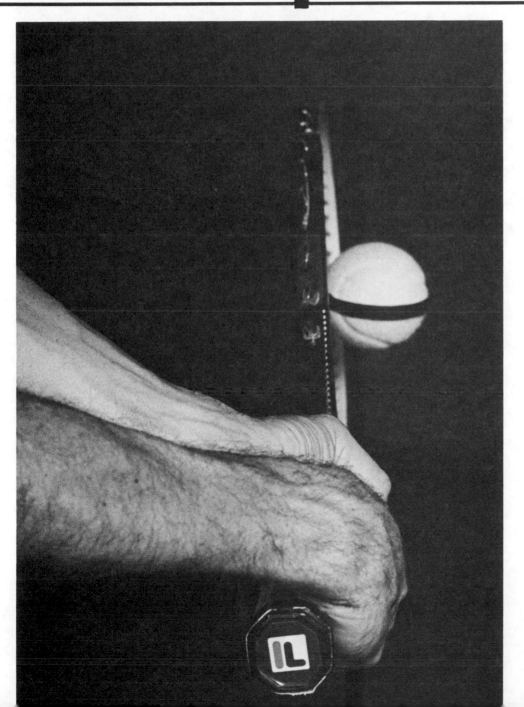

ow your hand holds the racket—your *grip*—can dramatically affect your tennis stroke and therefore your entire game. Some grips will help you to realize your full potential as a tennis player (functional grip), while other grips will prevent you from ever realizing your full potential (limiting grip). A superior athlete using a non-functional grip can become a very proficient tennis player, but it will be in spite of his limiting grip, not because of it.

If your intention is to become the best tennis player that you are capable of becoming, you must free yourself of any encumbrances and self-imposed handicaps by using functional rather than limiting grips.

FUNCTIONAL GRIP

A grip that is functional has the following characteristics:

It allows you the option of contacting the ball either *on* or *under* the equator, regardless of the height of the ball.

It allows the hand and wrist to be in a strong and comfortable position when the strings contact the ball *on* or *under* the equator.

It also allows the body to experience the most solid, pleasurable, and sensuous vibrations when contacting the ball.

LIMITING GRIPS

A grip that is limiting prevents you from tapping your true tennis potential because of the following:

1. It does not permit you the choice of contacting the ball *either* on or under the equator of the ball. This limits your contact options.
   a. Some grips cause you to incorrectly contact the ball on top of the equator. This will usually result in the ball flying into the net (an excessive Western Grip).
   b. Some grips cause the reverse problem—you *always* find yourself contacting the ball under the equator.

This usually results in a ball with a lot of spin but minimal power (Continental Grip).

2. It causes the hand and wrist to be in a weak and uncomfortable position when and if the strings ever contact the ball *on* the equator.
3. It does not permit the body to experience the most solid, pleasurable, and sensuous vibrations when contacting the ball. This is because an incorrect grip can cause a chopping or slicing motion.

LEARNING A NEW GRIP

Sometimes you will experience an immediate improvement with a new grip. More often, however, you will have to practice many repetitions before experiencing a breakthrough. Therefore, you must be extremely patient as you practice with a new grip. Impatience will lead to your prematurely abandoning what might eventually become a wonderfully functional grip. Note: If you are unwilling or unable to practice, it is usually unrealistic to learn a new grip because your body will probably never feel totally comfortable with it.

When learning a grip for the first time or when changing from an old to a new grip, do the following:

Rally more while playing fewer competitive sets. Your hand will usually slip back into its old limiting grip when playing in a competitive environment.

Hold the racket with the new grip while watching television and talking on the phone. (In order to get more comfortable with the new grip, your hand needs to touch the racket in a non-performance environment.)

Use a ball machine (slow speed) or a backboard. In both cases use gentle strokes.

Realize that the longer you have used the old grip, the more repetitions you need to do with the new grip.

Everyone must find the grip(s) that is right for him. Ultimately, everyone creates his own grip—one that is in harmony with the shape

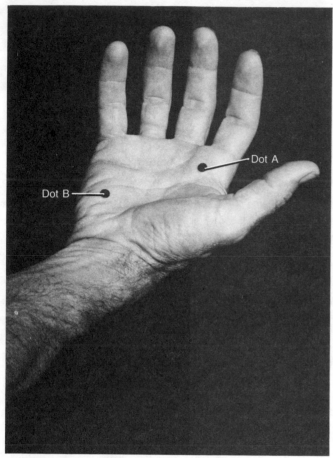
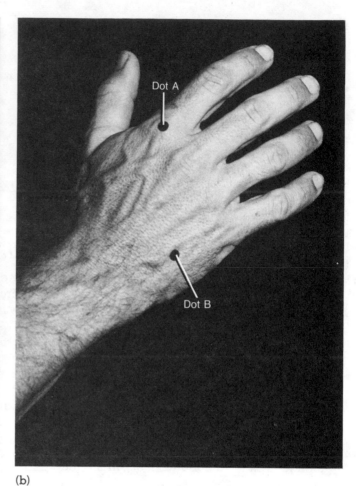

(a)   (b)

Figure 13-1
The two focal points—the palm knuckle (ball joint) and lower fleshy area—
(a) on the palm and (b) on the back of the hand.

and size of his hand, his athletic ability, and the shape of the handle of the racket. The information in this chapter was designed to help you find your grip.[1] The grip suggestions below will not apply to everyone. However, they should be applicable to at least 95 percent of the people reading this book.

The six different grips that will be discussed are the following:

1. Eastern Forehand Grip
2. Western Forehand Grip
3. Continental Forehand Grip

4. Eastern Backhand Grip
5. Continental Backhand Grip
6. Two-Handed Backhand Grip

The names of the above grips were coined a number of years ago. Whatever significance the names might have had is not particularly important now. Just think of these names as essentially arbitrary labels for each group.

If you are a beginner, I would suggest that you *first* focus your attention on the Eastern Grips and the Two-Handed Backhand grip.

The following information will be easiest to follow if you have a tennis racket with you when reading this chapter.

To properly understand how to create the

1. As you become more skilled and physically stronger, you might find that a grip that did not help you in the past now works very well for you.

above grips, there are two important focal points that must be discussed—the hand and the racket handle.

THE HAND

The palm contains two basic grip focal points: the palm knuckle (balljoint) of the index finger (dot A), and the lower fleshy area of the palm (dot B). The identical focal points are also indicated by dots A and B in their corresponding positions on the back of the hand. (See Figures 13–1a and b.)

THE RACKET HANDLE

Most racket handles have eight pronounced sides. By placing the strings at a right angle to the ground and looking clockwise, you can locate the eight sides. (See Figures 13–2a and b.)

1. The first flat, horizontal side of the handle is number one. Think of it as a highway that cars can drive on.

2. The second flat (slanting) side of the handle moving clockwise is number *two*. Think of it as a ski slope.

3. The third flat, vertical side of the handle is number *three*. Think of it as a vertical wall.

4. The fourth flat side is number *four*. It slants down and back under the handle. Think of it as the submerged hull of a ship.

5. The next important side is number *seven*. (It is opposite side three.) Think of it as the second vertical wall. This vertical wall is only important when creating a two-handed backhand.

Figure 13-2
The eight sides of a racket handle.

(a)

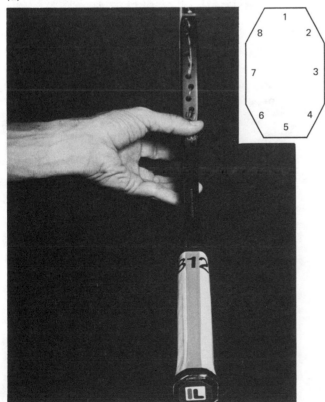

(b)

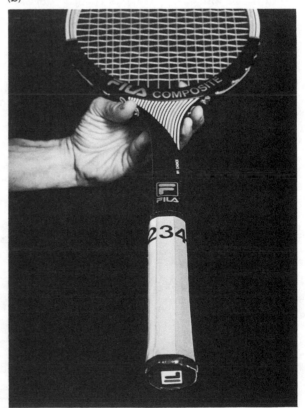

POSITIONING THE HAND ON THE RACKET

By placing dots A and B of your palm on different sides of the handle, you will be able to find all the major grips.

EASTERN FOREHAND GRIP

Both dots A and B touch middle portions of side number three. This grip naturally produces a flat racket face. The palm and strings are in a *vertical relationship* when the strings contact the equator of the ball. (See Figures 13–3a through d.) If you want the strings to touch under the equator, move the hand clockwise while keeping the same grip.

This is the most versatile forehand grip. It allows you to contact the ball on or under the equator regardless of the height of the ball.

WESTERN FOREHAND GRIP

Both dots A and B touch portions of side number four. The palm faces up, causing the strings to face down. (See Figures 13–4a through d.) The down-faced strings limit the usefulness of this grip to excessive topspin ground strokes. For the strings to touch *under* the equator of the ball, as would be necessary if the ball were very low, the wrist must be placed in an unnatural, and sometimes uncomfortable position.

Unless you are an advanced player, the Western Grip tends to be a limiting grip for the following reasons:

Since the face of the racket is naturally facing down (closed), there is a good chance that the strings will contact the ball on top of the equator, sending the ball into the net.

With the racket facing down, it is more difficult to return low balls because balls that are low must be contacted on or under the equator.

High balls (above the head) are also hard to return because stroke production at this height is difficult. The hand, wrist, arm, and shoulder tend to be in an awkward position.

When using this grip, be sure that the strings contact the ball on the equator, not on top of the equator. Sometimes it is helpful to imagine that you want to contact the ball *under* the equator (impossible with a closed racket face) in order to contact the ball on the equator.

If too many of your balls are going into the net when you use a Western Grip, experiment with a Semi-Western Grip. For a Semi-Western Grip, dots A and B are still located on side four, but are now much closer to side three.

The main advantage of a Western or Semi-Western Grip is that they both facilitate the production of topspin.

CONTINENTAL FOREHAND GRIP

Both dots A and B touch portions of side number two. (See Figures 13–5a through d.) This grip is most effective when used as a service and a forehand volley grip.

The grip naturally creates an open (up) racket face; the strings contact the ball under the equator. The palm and strings, at moment of contact, *naturally* face up, not flat or down. Unless you are a gifted player, you might have difficulty with this grip on forehand ground strokes for the following reasons:

In order for the strings to touch on the equator of the ball, the palm and wrist must assume a somewhat awkward position.

Since the strings are naturally open-faced, many players tend to contact the ball under the equator of the ball causing it to travel in a high arc, usually with backspin or sidespin. It is therefore difficult to produce an offensive forehand with this grip.

Contacting the ball on the equator places the arm in an extended locked position when the ball is at a height below the knees.

While backspin is easy to produce, flat and topspin shots are more difficult to produce.

It is difficult to return balls hit high to your forehand side.

Down-the-line shots are usually more difficult to produce than cross-court shots.

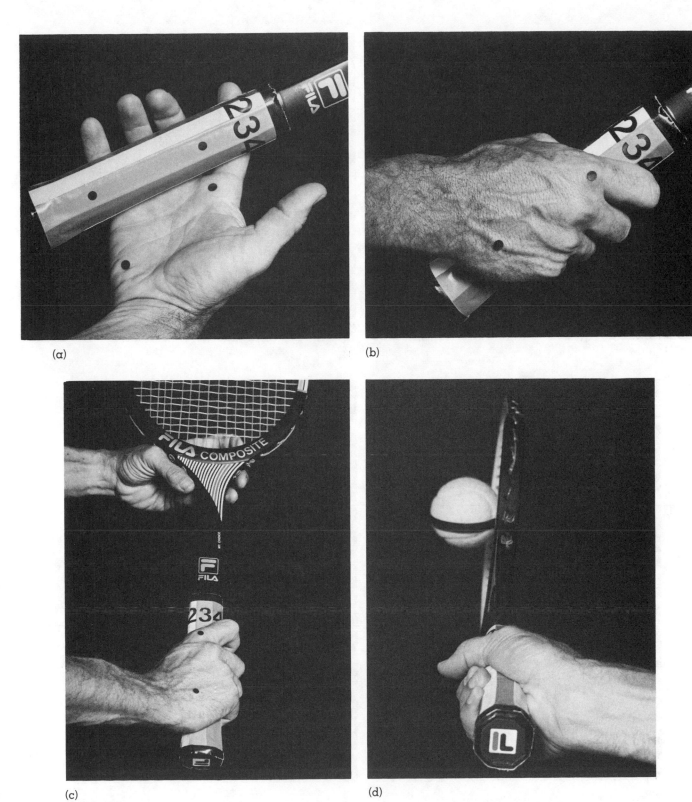

(a)

(b)

(c)

(d)

Figure 13-3
The Eastern Forehand Grip from various angles.

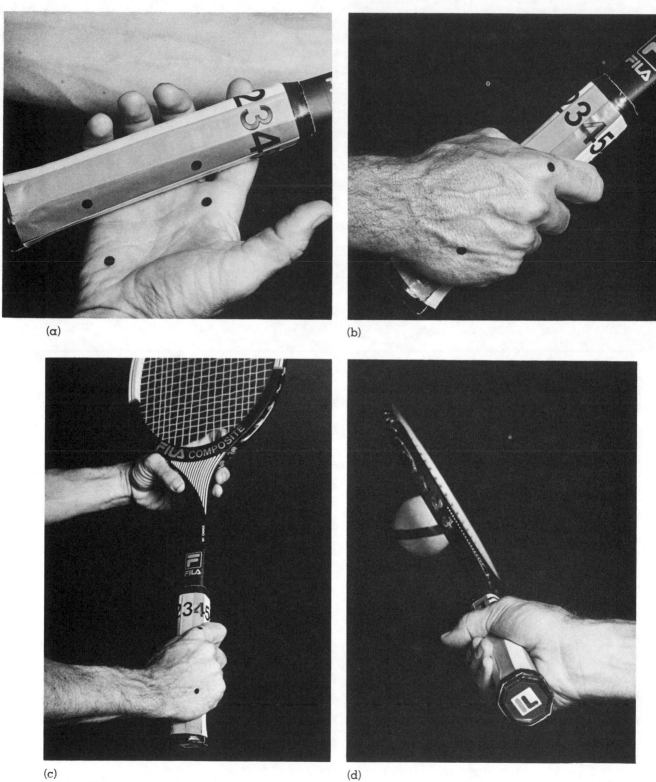

(a)

(b)

(c)

(d)

Figure 13-4
The Western Forehand Grip from various angles.

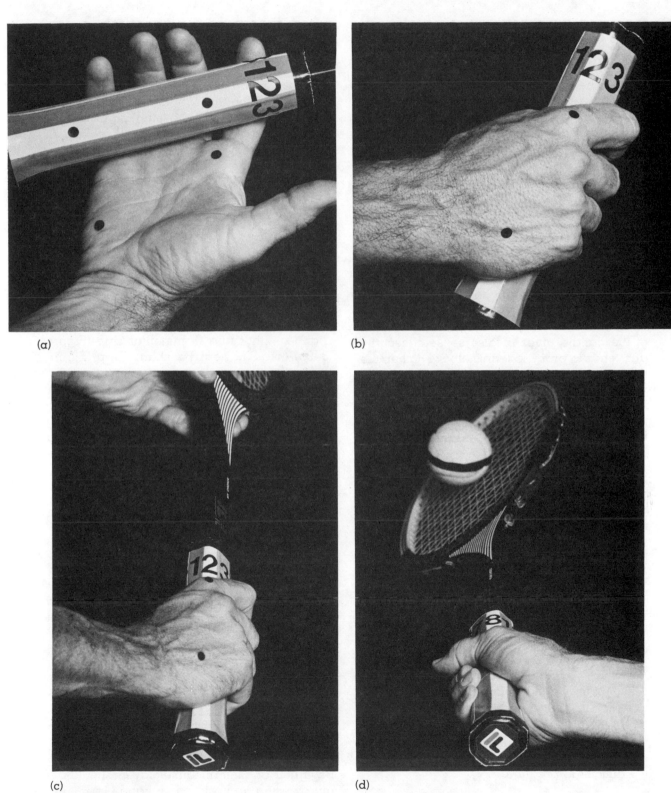

(a)

(b)

(c)

(d)

Figure 13-5
The Continental Forehand Grip from various angles.

EASTERN BACKHAND GRIP

Dot A touches the edge or ridge connecting side number one to side number two. Dot B touches near the middle of side number one. (See Figures 13–6a through d.)

This is the most versatile one-handed backhand grip. It allows you to contact the ball on or under the equator regardless of the height of the ball.

The Eastern Backhand Grip, like the Eastern Forehand Grip, naturally creates a flat-faced racket. If you want the strings to touch under the equator, the hand can slightly turn up (open faced racket) while keeping the same grip.

When creating a one-handed backhand (regardless of your grip), do not let your thumb rest directly on the seventh side (vertical wall) of the racket. Having the thumb "up the back" of the handle gives a false sense of security and tends to promote tennis elbow. Rather, the thumb should be wrapped *around* the handle when producing all one-handed backhands.

CONTINENTAL BACKHAND GRIP

This grip is the same as the Continental Forehand Grip previously described. Both dots A and B touch portions of side number two. This grip naturally creates an open-faced (up) racket. (See Figures 13–7a through d.)

Unless you are a gifted player, this backhand grip usually causes difficulties with backhand ground strokes for the following reasons:

In order for the strings to contact on the equator of the ball, the wrist must assume a weak, bent and awkward position.

Because the strings are naturally open-faced, you tend to contact under the equator of the ball, causing a weak, sliced shot. It is difficult to produce an offensive backhand stroke with this grip.

Although backspin or sidespin shots are easy to produce, flat and topspin shots are difficult to produce.

This grip is most effective when used as a backhand volley grip.

TWO-HANDED BACKHAND GRIP

Both hands are on the handle of the racket, with the left hand higher than the right hand. Both hands use the Eastern Forehand Grip. Dots A and B on the right hand touch number three. Dots A and B on the left hand touch side number seven (opposite side three). Both palms are on the same vertical plane as the strings when the ball is contacted on the equator. (See Figures 13–8a through e.)

These two Eastern Forehand Grips naturally create a flat faced racket and also allow you to contact under the equator of the ball.

MODIFIED TWO-HANDED BACKHAND GRIP

For this modified grip position, the *right* hand changes either to a Continental Grip (Figure 13–9a) or an Eastern Backhand Grip (Figure 13–9b). The left hand continues using the Eastern Forehand Grip.

The main advantage to this modified grip is apparent on those occasions when you have to reach wide for a ball, causing the left hand to leave the racket handle. When this is necessary, a modified grip will allow the right hand and wrist to be in a more secure and comfortable position when contacting the ball.

The disadvantages of the modified grip are:

The *right* hand must now change grips each time the ball comes to the backhand.

Excessively angular cross-court shots are more difficult to produce, because the right wrist tends to be in too restricted a position. This is especially true for the modified Eastern Backhand Grip (Figure 13–9b.)

GRIP SUGGESTIONS

FOREHAND GROUND STROKE

Beginners and intermediate players should begin by using an Eastern Forehand Grip.

Advanced intermediate and advanced players should use either an Eastern Forehand

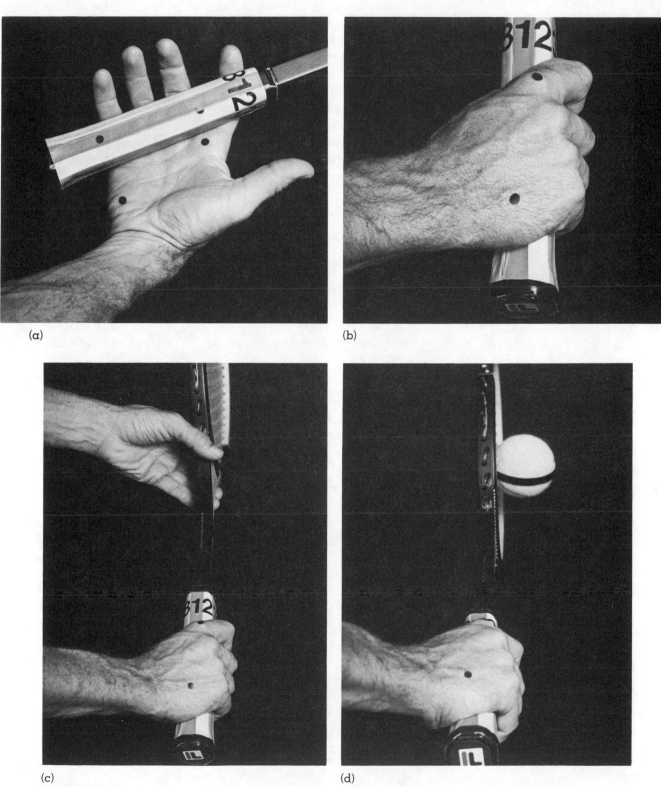

(a)

(b)

(c)

(d)

Figure 13-6
The Eastern backhand grip from various angles.

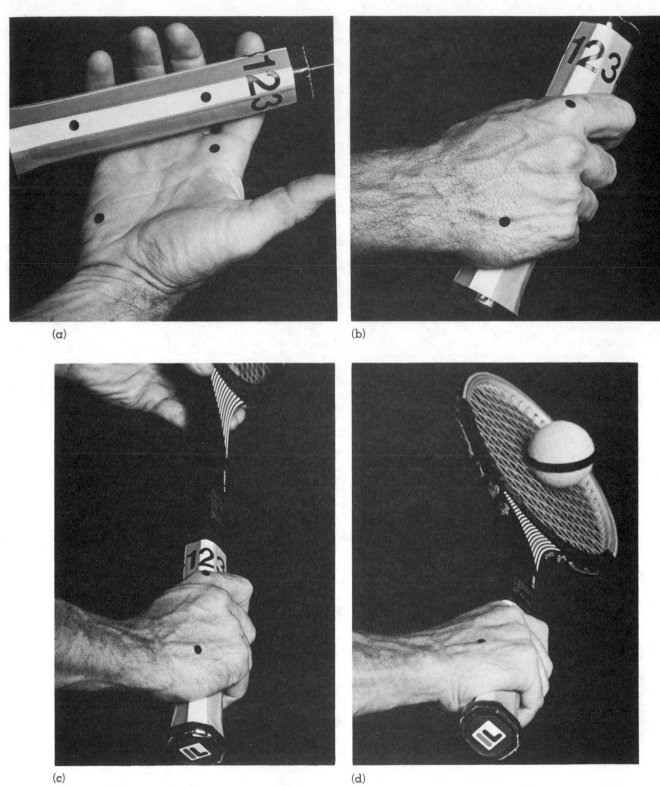

(a)

(b)

(c)

(d)

Figure 13-7
The Continental backhand grip from various angles.

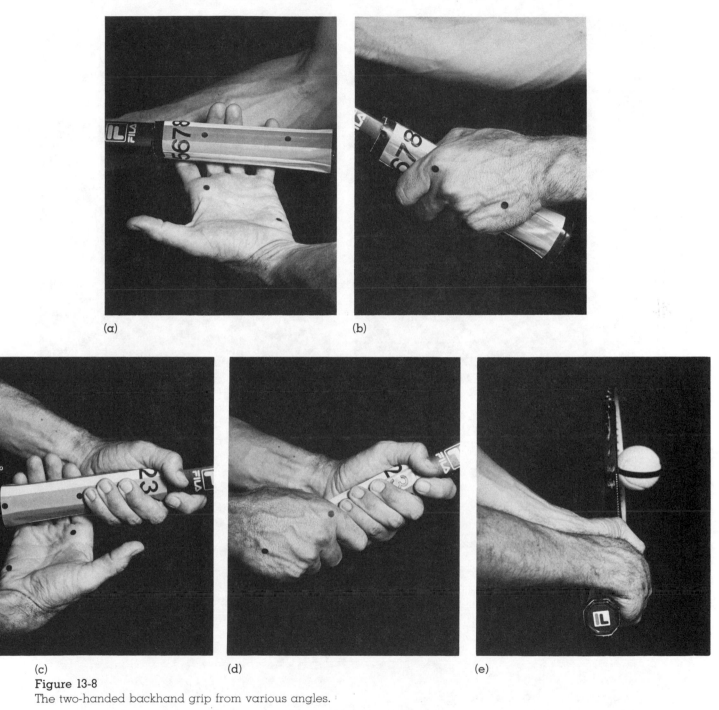

(a)

(b)

(c)

(d)

(e)

Figure 13-8
The two-handed backhand grip from various angles.

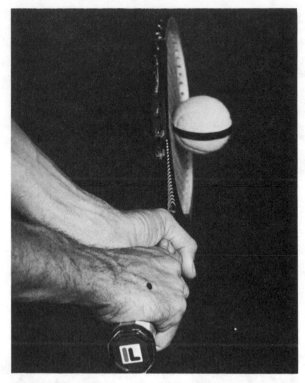 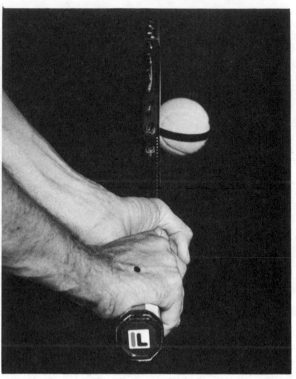

(a)   (b)

Figure 13-9
The modified Two-Handed Backhand Grip.

Grip of a Semi-Western Forehand Grip. A Western Forehand Grip should only be used by very advanced players.

BACKHAND GROUND STROKE

One-Handed Backhand

Beginners through advanced players should first learn the Eastern Backhand Grip, which will help produce a powerful and solid stroke. The Continental Backhand Grip will produce a stroke with more backspin, and beginners usually do not find it too functional.

Two-Handed Backhand

Beginners should first learn the regular Two-Handed Backhand Grip. After this grip becomes comfortable, the beginner can experiment with the modified Two-Handed Backhand Grip.

Intermediates and advanced players can immediately try all types of two-handed backhand grips to see which one feels most comfortable.

VOLLEY

Because time is of the essence when you are at the net, try to use the *same grip* for both Forehand and Backhand volleys (the Continental Grip).

If the Continental Grip is too uncomfortable, only then should you use your regular ground stroke grips for both forehand and backhand volleys. You'll lose time, but at least you'll be more comfortable when contacting the ball.

SERVE

Most advanced players use the Continental Grip when serving. This grip allows the player to produce both flat and spin serves with the most ease. Many beginners and intermediates, however, find that serving becomes more difficult when using the Continental Grip. If the Continental Grip does not come easily to you, and you don't have time to practice your serve, I would suggest that you serve with your regular forehand grip (or any other grip that you feel comfortable using).

Footwork

How you move your legs and feet on a tennis court is an important aspect of the game. Unfortunately, there is no universally agreed-upon system for learning or executing footwork. In fact, every teacher has his or her own method. Some teachers will program each step you take (some go as far as painting footprints on the tennis court), while others will rarely even mention the subject.

The problem with programming each step is that unless you practice these "step routines" several times a week, they will never feel totally organic to you. Your footwork will always be an intellectual, uncomfortable, and programmed experience. This tedious, technical, and robot-like approach has driven many players away from learning tennis.

The problem with *not* thinking about footwork at all is that you risk:

getting to the ball late,

being off balance when contacting the ball,

being unable to produce a long linear section,

being too slow returning to the ready alert position, and

being in a situation where your weight is committed in the wrong direction when your opponent hits the ball.

My approach to footwork is somewhere in the middle of the above all-or-nothing approaches. It is based on two major principles: that learning and executing all areas of footwork should be enjoyable, and that the footwork used should be functional.

As I see it, there are bascially three different major areas of footwork: running to the ball, positioning the feet for moment of contact, and moving back into position to await your opponent's return.

RUNNING TO THE BALL

If you were crossing the street and a truck traveling at sixty miles per hour were coming at you, you would not formulate a "correct" or "proper" way to move your feet. You would just run as fast as you could to the other side of the street. Your running form would be unimportant as long as you arrived at your destination alive.

So too with tennis. Getting to your destination on time is more important than your style of getting there. While I do not want you to worry too much about the exact way you are running, there are a few helpful preparation and running hints that you should keep in mind:

Wait in a *stationary position* for your opponent's return with your weight *equally distributed* between both feet. The legs should be spread fairly wide apart. As your opponent contacts the ball, make sure you are well-balanced and that your weight is not committed to any direction.

As your opponent contacts the ball, be on the balls of your feet, rather than on your heels.

Once you determine the path of your opponent's ball, run directly to the correct contact position along this projected path. Remember, the shortest distance between two points is a straight line.

POSITIONING THE FEET FOR MOMENT OF CONTACT

Just before, during, and after your moment of contact the body should remain well-balanced, regardless of whether you are stationary or in motion. Professional tennis players, roller skaters, dancers, unicyclists, tight rope walkers, etc., make their crafts seem easy because their bodies are always well balanced even though they are in motion. What is balance and how can you improve yours?

Imagine that there is a line or a stick that bisects the body, running from above the forehead to below the groin. This line is your vertical axis. Your center of gravity runs somewhere along this line. *Balance is the stability and comfort that are achieved when weight is evenly distributed on each side of the vertical axis.*

To achieve a more balanced stationary tennis stance do two things:

---

1. Before, during, and after contact, create a wide base (a minimum of two feet) between your feet. A wide base will improve your balance. (Think of the base of a pyramid to help you visualize the wide nature of your base.)

2. Do most of your bending from the knees, not the waist. Bent knees at moment of contact will lower your center of gravity and give you a more balanced base.

If the above suggestions seem too complicated, don't worry. The point is simply to try to remain in a balanced and pleasurable state throughout the entire tennis stroke. If you must be in motion, maintain your balance. *Balance at moment of contact should always take priority over complicated footwork.*

If you also don't like thinking about balance—relax. Just run to the ball any way you can and focus most of your attention on directing the ball with your hand. The more proficient your hand becomes, the less specific and perfect your footwork will need to be.

THE MOST POPULAR FOOTWORK POSITIONS

The following section has been created for players who need or want to know more about specific footwork. If you are satisfied with your current footwork you can skip this entire section.

If time permits, contact the ball from one of the following four stationary positions:

1. The long position,
2. The diagonal (semi-long) position,
3. The cross-over position, or
4. The wide position.

Tournament players during a set will usually use all four types of positions. Their choices are usually determined by three factors.

1. *Personal Physical Preference.* Some players are more comfortable using one type of footwork the majority of the time.
2. *Distance Away from the Approaching Ball.* If a player is afraid he won't reach a ball in time, he will use a footwork position that maximizes his reach.

3. *Distance to Travel When Returning to the Ready Alert Waiting Position.* When a player knows he must return quickly into the proper court area, he will use a stance at moment of contact that keeps his weight less committed (more evenly-balanced) rather than a stance that commits his weight too much in one direction.

If you are just learning tennis or are dissatisfied with your current footwork, I'd suggest you do the following: Try to develop the *long position* first. If executed correctly the long position will help promote the four most important characteristics of good footwork. If executed incorrectly, you will produce either the diagonal or cross-over step, both of which are also acceptable. The long position is especially helpful in promoting the creation of a long linear section.

Unless you are an advanced player, or someone who just loves the wide stance, I would suggest *not* learning it first because it tends to promote bad habits, causing most players to:

create circular, non-linear strokes,

push the ball forward rather than "carry" the ball forward,

slap at the ball by using too much wrist, and

use too much arm and not enough natural body motion.

The Long Position

The singles sideline and the doubles alley run the length of the court. In the long position the feet form an imaginary line that runs parallel to these sidelines. The long position for the forehand is created by the *left* foot stepping forward. This step transfers the weight onto the left foot *before* contact occurs. The long position for the backhand is created by the *right* foot stepping forward. This step transfers the weight on the right foot *before* contact occurs. (See Figures 14–1a through c.)

The advantages of this position are:

It is easy to create the linear section of the stroke because your balance can be maintained.

The long step forward facilitates the creation of topspin.

Figure 14-1
Create the long position
for the forehand by stepping forward
with the *left* foot.
(a)

Create the long position for the backhand
by stepping forward with the right foot.

(b)

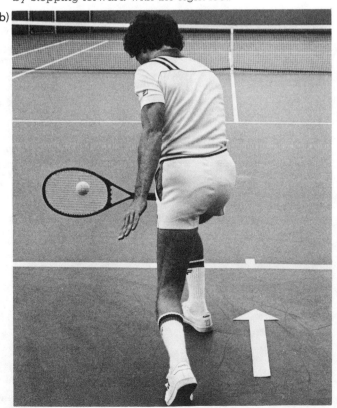

(c)

Figure 14-2
Create the diagonal (semi-long)
position for the forehand by
stepping toward the left net post
with the left foot.
(a)

Create the diagonal (semi-long) position
for the backhand by stepping toward
the right net post with the right foot.

(c)

(b)

Once your stroke is completed, the position allows you to move back quickly into the correct area of the court to await your opponent's next shot.

The main disadvantage of this position is that it is difficult to produce consistently. Even advanced players have difficulty producing a step that consistently runs parallel to the singles and doubles sidelines.

The Diagonal (Semi-Long) Position

The diagonal position is similar to the long position except that the final step is a little sideways (toward the net post) rather than exactly forward. The diagonal position for the forehand is created by the left foot stepping toward the left net post. Note that the outside portion of the foot, rather than the toe of the shoe, steps in the general direction of the post. This step transfers the weight onto the left foot *before* contact occurs. (See Figures 14–2a through c.)

The diagonal position of the backhand is created by the right foot (the outside portion of the foot) stepping toward the general direction of the right net post. This step transfers the weight onto the right foot *before* contact occurs.

The advantages of the diagonal (semi-long) position are:

It tends to be a fairly easy position to produce.

It allows for adjustment when the distance from the ball has been misjudged (for example, when you realize at the last instant that the long position will bring you *too* close to the ball).

It allows you to move back quickly into the correct area of the court to await your opponent's next shot, once you've completed your stroke.

The disadvantages of this position are:

It is a little harder to create strokes that incorporate long linear sections while still maintaining your balance.

Some players find it harder to generate enough power and/or fluidity when using this stance on the backhand side.

The Cross-Over Position

The cross-over position is created when one leg crosses over the other (similar to the cross-over-and-in step of the volley). The cross-over position for the forehand is created by the *left* leg stepping over the right leg and *forward*. As with the other positions, this step transfers the weight onto the left foot *before* contact occurs. The cross-over position for the backhand is created by the *right* leg stepping over the left leg and *forward*. This step transfers the weight onto the right foot *before* contact occurs. (See Figures 14–3a through c.)

The advantages of this position are:

This position offers you the greatest reach, especially in "emergencies" when you must get to a ball that is far from you.

You can create linear strokes and still maintain your balance.

When you try to create a long position and misjudge your distance from the ball, the cross-over position can be used to help you to get closer to the ball.

The main disadvantage is: at moment of contact your legs are crossed and your body weight and momentum are committed in the direction of the side fence. Recovering quickly from this position (after contacting the ball) can be difficult.

The Wide Position

The baseline runs the width of the court. In the wide position the feet are widely separated and parallel to the baseline. Many players refer to this position as the "open stance." In this position the navel faces the net. The wide position for the forehand is created by the *right* foot stepping sideways (to the right). This step for the forehand transfers the weight onto the *right* foot (rather than the left) *before* contact occurs.

The wide position for the *backhand* is created by the *left* foot stepping sideways (to the left). This step transfers the weight onto the left (rather than the right) *before* contact occurs. (See Figures 14–4a through c.)

You will notice that many top men professionals use the wide position stance on their forehands.

Figure 14-3
Create the cross-over position for the forehand by stepping over the right leg and forward with the left foot.
(a)

Create the cross-over position for the backhand by stepping over the left leg and forward with the right foot.
(c)

(b)

Figure 14-4
Create the wide position for the forehand
by stepping sideways (to the right) with
the right foot.
(a)

(b)
Create the wide position for the backhand
by stepping sideways (to the left)
with the left foot.

(c)

The main advantages to this position are:

Less time is required to prepare this footwork.

On the forehand side you can generate a powerful stroke, while preparing quickly.

Once your stroke is completed, you can quickly move your body in order to prepare for your opponent's next shot.

The texture of a clay court allows you to slide into a shot. The wide position helps you to maintain your balance and court position while sliding. (By lowering the knee that is furthest from the ball you can slow your slide down. Lowering the knee lowers the center of gravity, causing the body to slow down.)

The main disadvantages to this position are:

It is more difficult to create fluid linear strokes when your body is facing the net.

Some players find it harder to generate enough power and/or fluidity when using this stance on the backhand side.

For anatomical reasons, topspin is usually very difficult to create on the backhand side.

MOVING BACK INTO POSITION TO AWAIT YOUR OPPONENT'S RETURN

After contacting the ball, the most important factor to consider when moving back into the proper waiting position is the commitment of body weight. Just *before* your opponent contacts the ball it is very important to keep your weight neutral.[1] To accomplish this, the last few steps that you take should be side steps (or side shuffles). The side step is executed with your body facing the net. This step (even though it is slower than running) will enable you to move back into position with your weight in a relatively uncommitted and neutral position.

The only time you should run all the way back into position is when you are forced to contact the ball way off the court. In such a

case you need to run in order to cover a great distance in a short period of time. Unless you are way out of position, however, always try to use side steps as the final few steps that bring you back into your ready alert waiting position.

If your opponent is about to contact the ball and you have not yet reached your waiting destination—STOP!! Assume your ready alert waiting position even though you are *not* where you want to be. This stationary and neutral stance will still help you to get a very quick start when running after the next ball.

WHICH FOOTWORK POSITION IS BEST FOR YOU

You have just been introduced to four different possibilities for positioning the feet. You have also learned that each one has advantages and disadvantages. If you feel a little confused at this point, do not worry. The purpose of the preceding material was just to give you the full range of acceptable footwork.

Even if your footwork differs dramatically from the above mentioned, just make sure the stance you are using allows you to be:

balanced;

stationary (both feet remaining stationary) before, during, and after contact;

able to produce strokes with long linear sections; and

able to recover quickly.

If your current stance already contains the above four characteristics, I'd suggest that you stick with it. Trying to learn *new* footwork that you will feel comfortable using in a competitive situation takes patience and practice. Unless you are able and willing to practice new footwork (on the court or at home) it is unrealistic to dramatically change your current footwork.

In closing, just remember that the purpose of footwork, regardless of the stance you use, is to help you produce a stroke with pleasure and precision. Your footwork should never place your body in an uncomfortable position or jeopardize your moment of contact.

---

1. If you commit your weight to the left and your opponent contacts the ball and sends it to your right, your committed momentum will prevent you from quickly moving back to your right side.

chapter 15

Positioning

In singles, *where* you wait for the ball to be returned can mean the difference between always getting to the ball and rarely getting to the ball. Waiting in the correct spot can make you feel like a fast-moving advanced player, while waiting in the incorrect spot can make you feel like a slow-moving beginner.

YOUR OPPONENT'S POTENTIAL ANGLE

This entire positioning chapter will become very easy to understand once you understand the phrase "your opponent's potential angle." In Diagram 15–1 when your opponent (Y₁) is about to contact the ball, he has the option to direct the ball toward the middle of the court, to your right, or to your left. Leg YA of the angle represents his most consistent angular shot to your right side (from his perspective). Leg YB of the angle represents his most consistent angular shot to your left side. Angle AYB represents your opponent's potential angle. In more specific terms, what this means is that out of 1,000 successful shots, the odds are that *approximately* 950 (95 percent) will land somewhere in the area of angle AYB. The remaining 50 shots will land—intentionally or accidentally—in the shaded area. Because of their excessive angle, these shots will tend to be winners.

BISECT YOUR OPPONENT'S POTENTIAL ANGLE

Now that you understand the phrase "your opponent's potential angle," you will be able to follow the most important positioning rule in tennis. *Regardless of your opponent's position, always stand in a position that bisects his potential angle.* (See Diagrams 15–2 and 15–3.)

The size of your opponent's angle will vary depending on Y's proficiency. The more proficient Y is, the *smaller* the shaded area, and the *greater* Y's potential angle will be.

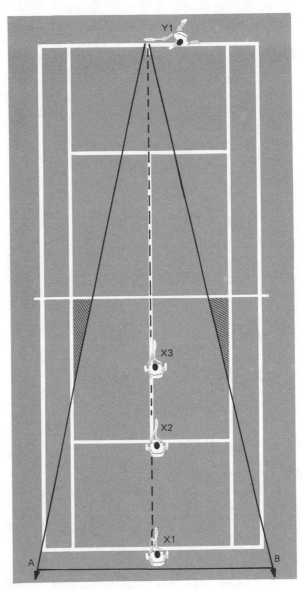

Diagram 15-1
Your opponent's potential angle.

CORRECT WAITING POSITION

Notice that in Diagram 15–1 X is always waiting in the middle of the court (X₁, X₂, X₃) to receive Y's shot. X₁, X₂, X₃ are all positions that bisect Y's potential angle. This is because Y happens to be positioned in the middle of the court. When Y changes positions, however, X must also change positions in order to bisect Y's potential angle (Diagrams 15–2 and 15–3).

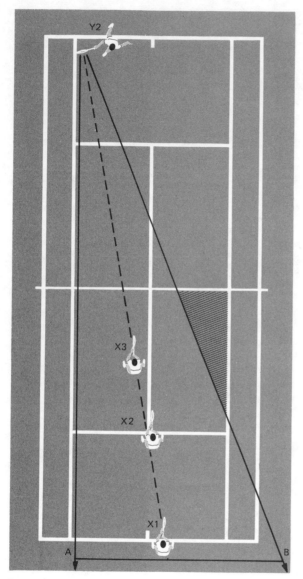

Diagram 15-2

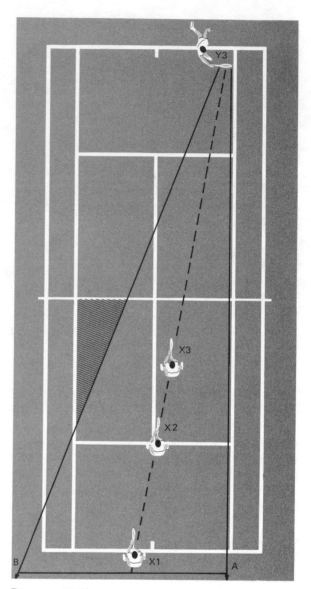

Diagram 15-3

Notice that in Diagrams 15–2 and 15–3, *leg B* of the angle (the variable leg) is always *expanding* away from X and toward the side fence. Therefore, in order for X to bisect Y's potential angle, X must position himself on one side of the court when waiting to return a baseline ground stroke (X_1), and on the other side of the court when waiting to return a volley near the net (X_3).

It is also interesting to observe that X_2 is in the same position in all diagrams. This is because X_2 is the only spot on the court that bisects Y's potential angle regardless of Y's position.

CORRECT WAITING POSITION SUMMARY

Taking the above information, we can make two general statements about your court positioning (when your opponent is at the baseline).

Figure 15-1
The correct waiting positions.

(a)

(b)

(c)

(d)

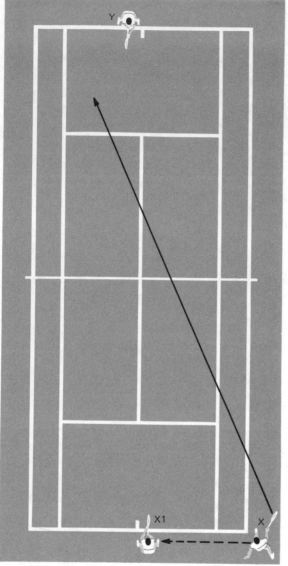

(a)

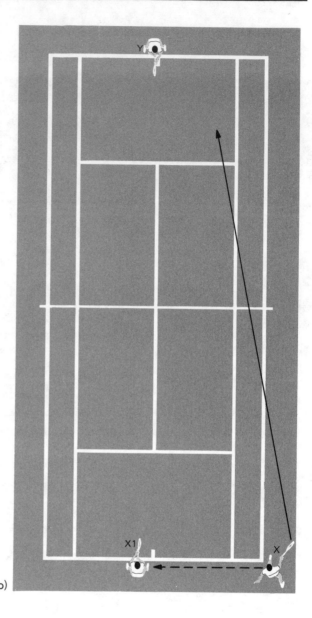

(b)

Diagram 15-4

1. When your opponent is about to contact the ball and you are at the baseline (X₁), wait on the *opposite side* of the court. (See Figures 15–1a and b.)

2. When your opponent is about to contact the ball and you are at the net (X₃), wait on the *same side* of the court as the one that he is on. (See Figures 15–1c and d.)

DIRECTING A BALL

We've just discussed your correct waiting positions when your opponent is about to contact the ball. We will next reverse our point of view and look at the most important factors that will help *you* determine where to direct the ball.

The major determining factor on where to direct the ball is *your* court position, and *not* your opponent's court position. (Unless you are going for a winning shot that your opponent cannot return.) Just before making a shot, a player should quickly go through the following decision making process. Eventually, these decisions will become an automatic and pleasurable part of your game.

If I make a cross-court shot, how far do I have to travel to get into the correct ready alert waiting position?

If I make a down-the-line shot, how far do I have to travel to get into the correct ready alert waiting position.

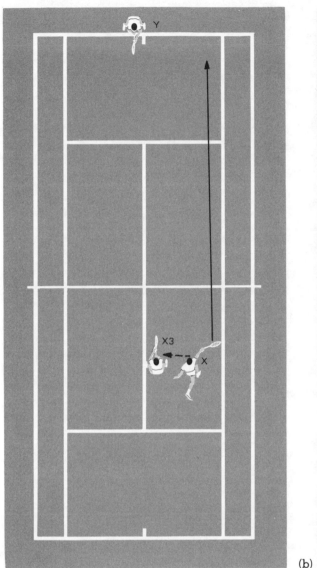

(a)

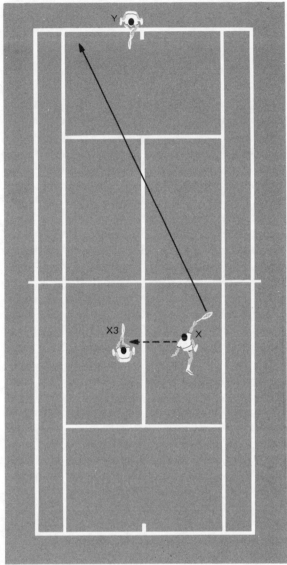

(b)

Diagram 15-5

In Diagrams 15–4a and b notice that X needs to travel a shorter distance after producing a cross-court shot than after producing a down-the-line shot. In Diagrams 15–5a and b, notice that when X is volleying, he needs to travel a shorter distance after producing a down-the-line shot than after producing a cross-court shot.

DIRECTING THE BALL SUMMARY

Taking the above information, we can make two general statements about directing the ball.

When at the baseline, by directing the ball cross-court you will have fewer steps to take to return to the correct waiting position (the position that will bisect your opponent's potential angle).

When at the net, by directing the ball down-the-line, you will have fewer steps to take to return to the correct waiting position (the position that will bisect your opponent's potential angle).

chapter 16

The Learning Process

Our bodies have the potential to absorb and understand any new craft, skill, or sport with amazing speed as long as a proper learning environment is created. Two of the most important ingredients of this learning environment are patience and proper practice methods.

> *The more time we invest in a sport,*
> *the more we expect from our performance.*
> *This performance expectation produces tension.*
> *Tension hampers the pleasure and precision process.*
>
> *Try instead to lower your performance expectation*
> *to that of a beginner, each time you play.*
> *This will permit your body more opportunity*
> *to fulfill its true athletic potential.*

THE ASSIMILATION PROCESS

It takes time for your body to absorb any new action. Just because you practiced one hundred serves yesterday, do not expect that your body has already absorbed and incorporated this new service action today. Sometimes it will take weeks or months before your body can fully absorb a new action.

Everyone assimilates new actions at different rates, but everyone can assimilate them. A big difference between a talented and less talented person is that the less talented person will require more repetitions before his body will assimilate the action. However, once the less talented person assimilates the action, it will be difficult to tell who is the more talented player.

When you do not put an "assimilation time table" on the absorption of a stroke, your body will be more relaxed and therefore more able to absorb the new action. To help speed up the assimilation process do the following:

Create a tensionless environment (place yourself in fewer competitive situations),

Practice the correct repetitions,

Keep the body free of tension when producing a pleasurable stroke.

BECOME A BEGINNER

Always think of yourself as a beginner whenever you play tennis, regardless of your level.

By becoming a beginner, your body can become tensionless and free of expectations. You will therefore permit your body to function at a high level of freedom.

The level of my game always sinks whenever I think of myself as a tennis professional, because then I do not give myself room to make errors or to have fun. When I enter the court as a beginner, however, I do not expect anything from my game. I can get back to the basic fundamentals of tennis: It is a game of two variables (the ball and the racket) and two constants (the net and the court). The strings must contact the ball so that it flies over the net and into my opponent's court.

How many times have you played great tennis on Saturday and poor tennis on Sunday? You probably foolishly thought on Sunday that you were an advanced player. After playing brilliant tennis, you must always become a beginner once again.

There is wisdom in the term "beginner's luck." You rarely bring any tension or expectation to a sport, craft, or skill the first time you try it. The second time, however, you already begin to bring expectations along with you. "If I did so well the first time, imagine what I will be able to do the second time." What you usually discover, however, is that you are doing worse the second time and enjoying the activity less. If you continue to pursue this sport, craft, or skill for many years, imagine how many expectations you can accumulate.

YOU WILL NEVER BE SATISFIED WITH YOUR GAME

Playing tennis should be as enjoyable as going for a nice walk. I'm sure that you would never turn to your spouse and say, "Don't talk to me today. I walked miserably this morning." Silly, isn't it? So what's so different about your tennis game? Why ruin an entire Sunday just because your game that morning was not up to snuff? You still got exercise, breathed fresh air (maybe), and played a game with a friend.

Start changing some of your goals in tennis so that you can always be a winner, regardless of the score.

> *Fear of imperfection is the curse of Mankind,*
> *for fear of imperfection kills the growth*
> *process. There is beauty and dignity in*
> *imperfection,*
> *for imperfection leaves us something to do*
> *for tomorrow.*

UNDERSTANDING YOUR STROKES

We perform hundreds of simple actions each day. We open doors, we tie our shoe laces, we turn faucets on and off. We execute these actions correctly again and again because our bodies fully understand them. There is no mystery or luck involved. Likewise, our goal in tennis is to understand each stroke as clearly as we understand each of our daily activities. If you are having problems with the consistency and accuracy of your strokes, slow them down until you understand the specific actions that are necessary to perform them correctly and organically.

APPLY ALL PAST EXPERIENCES TO TENNIS

Take most things that you have learned from other sports, skills, and art forms, and apply them to tennis. Do not think of tennis as an isolated and unique sport. For example, a skier should experience the same feeling of balance when he is contacting a tennis ball as when he is skiing. Likewise, a pianist should experience the same feeling of connection when he is contacting a tennis ball as when he is contacting the keys.

Isolation of Actions

When practicing (or when you need to relax during competition) concentrate on consciously performing only one action at a time. While your body will unconsciously be performing many actions, your mind should focus and concentrate on only one. *Don't think about the results of your stroke; rather, just execute the specific action.* If you worry about the results of your stroke (where the ball is going to land) your specific isolated action will be compromised. By concentrating on the specific action

and not on the result of that action, however, your body will learn to execute and integrate the desired action sooner, because the specific action was executed with greater purity and less tension.

Action: Bring the racket back *before* the ball bounces.

If you successfully bring the racket back before the ball bounces, be delighted with your stroke, even if you totally mis-hit the ball.

Action: At moment of contact, the shoulder and arm should be totally relaxed and in a pleasurable state.

If your shoulder and arm experience relaxation and pleasure at moment of contact, be happy with your stroke, even if your ball flies over the fence.

As soon as you change your *goal* priorities from results to *actions*, your strokes will improve much sooner. The specific and pleasurable execution of the action is always more important than the results of that action.

Slow Stroking Practice

An interesting story is told about Julius Baker, a member of the New York Philharmonic Orchestra and a great flutist. A friend, also a flutist, came to visit him at his home and heard Mr. Baker practicing. When the musical piece was completed, his friend said, "Julius, you and I know that that piece of music should be played much faster than you are playing it. Why are you playing it so slowly?" Mr. Baker's answer is said to have been, "If I practice the piece this slowly, my fingers never get a chance to practice any mistakes."

Similarly, when you practice your tennis strokes slowly, your body will learn the stroke pattern sooner. Your body and racket will have the time to produce the desired coordinated actions.

Slow practice allows your body to produce a stroke with little or no tension. Lack of tension permits your body to absorb the needed actions within the shortest period of time.

Opposite page: Figure 16-1
Tennis is an art form disguised as a sport.

It is also very difficult to work on stroke production when the oncoming ball is traveling fast. If you ever practice on a ball machine, set the machine at a slow speed. If you are rallying, ask the person on the other side of the net to slow down his or her shots for a while.

Slow, relaxed practicing creates the best environment within which to transform intellectual information into physical memory.

Your Body Has a Mind of Its Own

Last year I bought a stick shift car without the foggiest idea of how to drive it. Every time I drove I had so many things to think about that I almost went crazy. I could not even have the radio on or carry on a conversation. Every conscious second was spent on clutching and shifting or worrying about clutching and shifting.

A year has passed and I am now shifting without even thinking about it. My body is doing all of those very difficult actions automatically, as if it had a mind of its own. Anyone who has mastered a craft, skill, musical instrument, or sport has experienced this phenomenon.

If you want to experience what I'm talking about on a very simple level, do the following: Bend down and quickly untie your shoe lace and then quickly tie it again. Did you feel how your fingers, not you, tied them? Your fingers seemed to have a detached life and purpose of their own. They executed a programmed pattern of actions. This is called "muscle memory."

With many *correct* repetitions your tennis game can also reach a programmed pattern of actions. Your body can eventually coordinate and execute many actions, even when you are thinking about what to eat for dinner. At this skillful level of tennis, all *you* will need to do is to pick a place where you would like the ball to land and *your body* will do the rest. Only when a mistake is made will you consciously need to think of the necessary and specific actions that must accompany each stroke. Unfortunately, most people never do enough correct repetitions to ever reach this level, which is ironic because this level offers the player the highest and most addictive feeling a tennis player can experience.

INCORPORATING NEW ACTIONS INTO YOUR CURRENT TENNIS STROKE

When trying to incorporate new actions into your current tennis strokes, you should always remember that your body will never forget the old stroke pattern. Therefore, *never* try to break an old tennis stroke habit. The more you try to destroy an old habit, the more stubbornly it will persist. The way to incorporate new forms into your current tennis strokes is to practice the new actions realizing that your old ones will always be lurking somewhere in the shadows. Nurture the new habit, rather than trying to kill the old one.

Be aware that when placed in competitive and pressuring situations, your body will produce the stroke with which it is most comfortable and secure. Often this will be your old tennis stroke. You will know that your body has started to absorb the new actions when it uses the new stroking patterns under stress.

PRACTICING IN A NON-COMPETITIVE ENVIRONMENT

Whenever we play a set of tennis, the stakes always seem to be too high. Our entire skill and self-esteem are usually put on the line. Playing a set seduces both players into playing very competitively. In this highly competitive environment it becomes impossible to practice new stroke actions. Practicing new actions requires a non-competitive and safe environment. If you are truly interested in improving your strokes, *play fewer sets of tennis.*

If you insist on playing tennis competitively, competing partners might try a ping-pong scoring system. In this system each point counts as only one point. The first player scoring twenty-one points wins. Each server serves five points. First and second serves are allowed. Because this scoring system does not resemble a set of tennis, the thought of losing one of these games is not as devastating. Therefore, you will be able to practice your new stroke actions with more freedom.

PRACTICE EVERY DAY FOR FIFTEEN SECONDS

Just the *thought* of practicing anything is enough to depress most people. Notice that I did not say that practicing depresses us. It is the *thought* of it that is the most frightening part of the learning process. Once we become engaged in actual practice, however, most of the fear and dread either goes away or becomes secondary. If this practice fear becomes too overwhelming, we will never do it. What we must do in order to practice anything on a more consistent basis is to make this thought of practicing less painful.

Make the commitment to practice at least fifteen seconds *every day*.[1] At the end of fifteen seconds, decide whether you want to practice any more. If you decide that practicing more than fifteen seconds is too painful, stop for the day. But if you can practice a little more, just continue. What most people find is that they will rarely stop after fifteen seconds.

> *Time and correct repetitions breed familiarity and dissipate tension.*

1. (You do not need to be on a tennis court to practice. Refer to the Contact Chapter—Helpful Exercises to Improve the Moment of Contact.)

chapter 17

Competition

The information in this section was designed to help you produce pleasurable and precise tennis strokes when placed in a competitive environment. This information is also applicable to other performance related activities, such as public speaking, acting, dancing, and singing.

PERFORMING ON THE COURT

> *If you can meet with triumph and disaster, and treat those two imposters just the same...*
> *Rudyard Kipling*

The secret of winning is always to maintain the pleasure and precision priority. Unfortunately, when in competition, many players reverse the order of these words, as the importance of each stroke causes precision and tension to supersede pleasure and relaxation. *Great* competitors, on the other hand, dare to keep pleasure as their first priority even during the most important points. While a great competitor obviously needs a precise stroke, he is not willing to sacrifice fluidity and comfort for it. It is from this noncompromising stance that real mastery flows.

A Mental Movie of Victory

In the last several years a large body of research has been done in the area of the effects of mental rehearsal and visualization on performance. Scientists have found that if we make a mental movie of our victory, whatever insecurities we may feel during a match will not affect us so deeply. A small setback will be less likely to undermine our game.

Before your next match, use your imagination in the following manner. In the privacy of your home or office, create a mental movie of the highlights of your forthcoming victorious match. Have the camera capture you leaving your home, arriving at the court, and warming up. Include scenes of the last two points, both of which you win. See yourself running up to the net and shaking hands with the loser. See the final score up on the scoreboard. Congratulations!

How to Beat a Player Who Is Better Than You

Here is a helpful technique to help you gain the confidence to beat someone who you feel is better than you.

First, ask yourself what the phrase "better than I am" really means. You will probably find it means that your opponent will beat you more times than you will beat him.

Next, make believe that you and your opponent are going to play a set every day for a year. Now ask yourself, "How many times is this person going to beat me in a year?" If he is a lot better than you are, you might arrive at a figure of, let's say, 360. So, your opponent will win 360 times and you will win 5 times.

Suddenly, you have established the fact that you can in fact beat him. It might only be 5 times a year, but you now know that you can beat him. The only thing left to do is for you now to make today one of those 5 days.

What this technique does is allow both of you to keep your same "tennis identities." You know that he probably will always be better than you are *and* you are still going to beat him today. Every time you go on the court, *make today the day.*

Intention

Make sure that you are very clear about what your intention is before competing with someone. Do you really want to win? Many players who lose usually do so because they are not as clear and honest about their intention as their opponent is. Most top tennis matches, boxing matches, etc., go beyond a battle of skills. They are competitions of intention.

Make sure before you enter a tennis court that you are very clear about what you want to accomplish out on the court. There is nothing wrong with just wanting to give someone a run for his money. The problem arises when you lie to yourself about what you really intend to do. Be very honest and aware about your intentions and notice what happens on the court.

Preparing the Body Before Arriving at the Court

Proper preparation for a tennis game begins *before* you set foot on the court. Most players do not allow enough time for a leisurely and relaxed arrival at the tennis court. If you leave late and get caught in traffic, you will usually arrive at the court tense and frustrated. While in this state it is difficult to play well. To encourage yourself to play in a pleasurable and relaxed state do the following:

1. Enjoy the trip to the tennis court. Allow enough time. If driving, make sure you are not grabbing the steering wheel, which will produce a tense shoulder and neck.
2. Do gentle stretching and warm-up exercises before entering the court.
3. Before beginning to play, sit down on a chair, close your eyes, and do the following relaxation exercises.
   a. See if you can locate any tension in your body. Start at your head and work down to each of your toes. Specifically check every part of your body. Release any tension once it is located. See how loose your entire body can become. Let your muscles and bones feel like one huge piece of jello.
   b. Listen to all the sounds around you.
   c. Take several long, deep breaths.

Use Your Senses When Entering a Tennis Court

The more nervous you are, the more you should use your senses when entering the tennis court. Using the senses helps to reduce tension, allowing the body to function to its full capacity.[1] Do only one "sensory exercise" at a time.

1. *Sense of Touch:* Touch the surface of the court. The rougher the surface, the slower the ball will travel once it

bounces (more friction between the ball and the ground).
2. *Sense of Sight:* Look at the court, the net, and the balls. If you are outdoors, determine which way the wind is blowing by checking a flag or by observing which way a small part of a leaf falls when it is dropped.
3. *Sense of Hearing:* Listen to all of the sounds around you. When rallying, listen to the sound that is created when your opponent contacts the ball. This sound can give you a lot of information as to the speed and amount of spin on the ball.
4. *Sense of Smell:* What can you smell while on the tennis court?

Pre-Game Jitters

If you find you are nervous while warming-up and/or when the game begins, just remember one thing: Chances are that your opponent is also nervous. So there you have two scared, grown-up people on a tennis court with a net separating them. Save some energy. If he or she is scared, there is no reason for you also to be scared. Let your opponent be scared for both of you.

A boxer has reason to be afraid of his opponent, but you do not. Your opponent cannot come over to your side of the court. Also remember that the ball is *not* your opponent. It is not alive nor does it belong to your opponent. It is just a hollow piece of rubber covered with material. It flies back and forth over the net.

Just before the first point begins, look over at your opponent and in a very low voice say— *BOO!!!*

You Are Only Human

Whenever you enter a tennis court, be sure that you are not immediately demanding perfection of yourself. Recognize that you have not played tennis for a day, or longer, that your body is not warmed-up, and that you will make many mistakes before getting properly attuned. Give yourself the liberty to be human. Go for pleasurable strokes rather than perfect

---

1. Sensory work encourages you to live more in the present and less in the past or future.

strokes. Let pleasure be the "constant" ingredient and precision be the "variable" ingredient. A system that has helped me very much is the following:

> While warming up, I allow myself twelve stupid, embarrassing mistakes before I even start to get bothered.
>
> While playing the match I will allow myself eight of the most humiliating shots ever produced before I even begin to get annoyed.

By allowing myself these mistakes, I make fewer of them. Once again, *by letting nothing interfere with my pleasure*, I leave the body free to perform with greater proficiency. We will always have imperfection in our lives, so why let imperfection negate pleasure?

> *Tension, not your opponent, is your greatest enemy on the court.*

Your Opponent Is Your Partner

Thinking of the person on the other side of the net as your *opponent* usually does more harm than good.

Whenever someone *opposes* us, we tend to become tense, serious, rigid, impatient, annoyed at imperfection, and nervous—which does not let the body function at optimum level. You will find that your body performs with much more pleasure and precision and much less tension if you turn your opponent into a kind of partner. A partner is someone who plays on the same team or side with another. You work with a partner, though you both have different functions to perform while on the court.

Functions of Your Partner
Your "partner's" function is to chase after the balls and to stroke them back to your side. He performs this function for free.

As part of this "team effort," only your "partner" should become tense, serious, rigid, impatient, and annoyed at his own imperfection.

Another function falling to your "partner" is to lose. Even as he starts to win, do not fret; his function is to lose, regardless of how he likes to scare you.

Your Functions
To enjoy being on the court and stroking each ball.
To win.

Turning your opponent into your "partner" will allow you to combine his energy with yours. Suddenly, these forces join together in a synergistic fashion. Both he and you are working together to enable *you to win*.

Perform Specific Actions

Whenever you become nervous while playing, perform *specific actions*. The execution of these actions will shift your attention away from your nervousness. Following is a list of some of these actions:

1. Focus Your Eyes on the Ball:
   a. *Try* to see the ball as it leaves your opponent's strings, as it lands on your side, and as it contacts your strings.
   b. *Try* to read what brand name is written on the ball as it approaches you.

2. Breathe:
   Start to breathe in slowly and gently just before, during, and just after contacting the ball. Receiving air will remind you to receive pleasure. Breathing in will also help to keep the shoulder free and relaxed at moment of contact. (If breathing in feels awkward, try slowly and gently breathing out.)

3. Sing a Song:
   Singing (softly) during a point (or in between points) will remind you that enjoyment is the most important part of tennis. While in this musical state you will discover that the body will usually make fewer errors.

4. Execute Sensory Actions:
   To alleviate tension do your sensory actions (previously mentioned) in between points.

Figure 17-1a
STEWART CONSTIPADA

Figure 17-1b
SCARLATO VINDICTA

Limitations

When playing competitively against a player who appears to be on your level or higher, it is imperative that you recognize and accept your own limitations as a player. In competition, do not become the kind of tennis player you would like to be. Do not go for shots you would like to be able to make. Rather, become the kind of player you are. Go for the shots that you can consistently deliver. You will become a much more formidable opponent when you perform excellently at your present level.

The Real Opponent

In tennis you do not have to worry about playing well as long as you can force your opponent into playing poorly. That is why so many steady players (who might have terrible-looking form) win a lot of matches. They are totally focused on getting the ball back over the net and on giving their opponent another chance to make a mistake. The other player

gets frustrated and begins to attempt low percentage (non-statistical) shots. He begins to make errors. These errors infuriate him, and he plays even more poorly. He has now become his own opponent.

When you play a match, be sure not to become your own opponent. You must be in harmony with yourself in order to force your opponent into playing poorly.

Never put pressure on yourself to play well. Put pressure on your opponent to play poorly.

"Becoming"

Do you envy the confidence and poise of the top pros as they enter the tennis court and begin to play? If so, you can incorporate these same personal characteristics into your own court entrance and game through a process called "becoming." It allows you to tap the confidence, poise, etc. of another person, by actually believing that you are that person. Become that person by taking on his/her at-

Figure 17-1c
WEMBLEG WARRINGTON III

Figure 17-1d
CORZU CAMACHO

titude, walk, posture, etc. Take on these characteristics through relaxation and not tension. Be sure to *feel* like that person, rather than acting out a superficial non-feeling characterization. When becoming, be sure to use only one person at a time as your model.

Disguises

When we play a tennis match, we somehow believe our name is at stake. We cannot take risks for fear of tarnishing our "family crest." Losing feels as if a part of us were being put to death. To lessen this fear, enter a tournament or play a match in an area where you are not known. If no one knows you, the stakes will become lower. To diminish the chances that your ego will emerge, you can also wear a disguise and change your name. A weird hat, dark shades, a mustache, or a crazy jacket are some suggestions.

A story is told about the old and great Japanese master painters. To preserve their artistic growth and to down-play their egos,

they were required to change their names every five years. With a new name they had nothing to live up to, so they were able to risk, experiment, fail, and ultimately grow to new heights.

Disguises and name changes can free you to discover new paths to your identity and potential. (See Figures 17–1a through d.)

DEVELOPING A COMPETITIVE STRATEGY

> *When one is in action*
> *One does not have fear.*
> —Charles Lindbergh

The information in this section was designed to help you become a better competitor by observing your opponent's patterns and habits and by using your strokes in a more effective manner.

Some Things to Observe About Your Opponent's Game While Warming Up

Is he a right- or left-handed player? Sometimes we get so excited or nervous that we neglect to observe that our opponent is a left-handed player, which would mean that what you thought was his backhand side is actually his forehand side.

Does your opponent hit the ball gently or with power? If he uses a lot of power, there is a chance that his strokes are inconsistent. When the game begins, try to keep the ball in play rather than going for outright winners. Let him make the first mistake.

Is one of his sides noticeably weaker than the other? If so, send the ball to his weaker side when approaching the net.

Send your opponent a short, shallow ball. Observe where he goes after he returns it. If he runs back to the baseline rather than up to the net area, he is probably more comfortable with his baseline game than his volley game. During a game, therefore, try to force him up to the net by hitting shallow balls, including drop shots.

While your opponent warms up his volley, see if he crosses one leg over the other to reach the ball. If he does, he maximizes his reach. If, instead, he side-steps to the ball, it will be easier for you to send balls past him because his reach will be limited. (See The Volley Chapter for a more detailed explanation.)

Assume your opponent is not comfortable with a stroke he does not warm up. In other words, if he does not warm up his overhead smash, or volley, assume these strokes will be weak.

Observe your opponent's speed. How fast is he? Do you think he will tire easily? If so, move him around the court. Bring him up to net and lob over his head. Force him to burn up energy.

Is your opponent able to hit sharp cross-court angular shots? If so, do not give him the opportunity. Direct your balls into the middle of the large back-court box. He will have more difficulty producing this sharp angular shot from the center of the court.

Game Plan Goals

To try to enjoy every second on the court (regardless of the score).

To keep the body in a relaxed state every time you contact the ball.

To keep the ball in play and not to attempt any outright winners.

To force your opponent to contact each ball when he is standing outside of the singles court (either behind the baseline or wide of the singles side line).

To choose targets that are at least two to three feet within your opponent's court. In this way you provide a margin of error should your stroke be a few feet off.

To have each shot clear the net by several feet (assuming your opponent is not playing the net). A high clearance of the net provides you with a margin for error.

To force your opponent to be in an off-balanced position each time he contacts the ball.

To have only one target when your strokes are off—the middle of the large, back-court box.

To throw your opponent's rhythm off by mixing up the speed and spins of your shots.

Use only one game plan at a time. It is very difficult to combine game plans and still keep your focus and concentration.

Helpful Hints Once the Game Begins

Keep a winning game. Change a losing game. If something works for you, keep doing it. Don't get fancy and add frills. If you are losing, shake up the mix. Go in the opposite direction. Experiment. Use another strategy.

Do not imitate your opponent's style of play unless you are better at it than he is.

Unless you are a tournament player, do *not* meet power with power. If your opponent hits you a very fast ball, don't try to add any more speed. Rather, try to use the speed of your opponent's ball as your primary energy source. This can be accomplished by shortening your backswing and by keeping your shoulder relaxed during the stroke.

Do not adopt your opponent's emotional approach to the sport. If he plays a very serious and tense game, do not be seduced into playing *his* way. Dance to your own kind of music.

During a match, return a hard-hit ball in the direction from which it came. Your timing at moment of contact becomes twice as difficult when you try to change the angle of a hard-hit ball. Thus, if your opponent sends a hard-hit cross-court shot to you, return the ball cross-court.

Direct a majority of your shots cross-court. The net is lower and your target area is larger cross-court than down-the-line. (See Positioning Chapter for further information on cross-court shots.)

Some player's strokes look strong during warm-up, but fall apart as soon as the first point begins. Make sure to test out your opponent's forehand and backhand strokes as soon you begin playing.

When playing against a steady "dinker" (someone who hits very gently), force him to come to net by hitting shallow balls or drop shots. Once he is at net, lob over his head, pass him, or force him to volley the ball below the height of the net. Most "dinkers" have poor overhead smashes and volleys.

To Serve First or Not to Serve First

One of the standard assumptions of tennis is that the server should win his service game. This thought puts an enormous amount of pressure on the server. One technique to try, therefore, is to have your opponent serve first (especially when you are nervous). Suddenly, all of the psychological pressure of serving well and winning the first game falls onto your opponent.

If you decide to serve first, concentrate on creating a successful first serve. This will put immediate pressure on your opponent to perform. Do *not* try to ace or overpower your opponent on the first serve, especially when you are nervous. Pleasure the serve, don't power it.

Competing Against a Poorer Player

Have you ever noticed how poorly you play when you compete against a poorer tennis player? More often than not, your game just falls apart, leaving two "beginners" who scratch and claw their way through a set or match. Playing someone who isn't as proficient as you are can be one of the most painful experiences of your life.

Here is a list of helpful hints for you when playing someone whose tennis game isn't as good as yours:

Your major goal must be to enjoy the experience. You have to be on the court, so why not enjoy it. Take this as an opportunity to practice the relaxed and pleasurable approach to tennis you've been introduced to in this book.

To lower your expectations, make believe you are a beginner. Do *not* think of yourself as an advanced player who is about to destroy his opponent.

Become a patient tennis player. Try to keep the ball in play rather than to immediately win each point.

Gently add additional power to the ball. Do not add an enormous amount of power all at once.

Since your opponent's game probably has no rhythm, create your own and flow with it.

Do not feel sorry for your opponent. Do not purposefully lose any games unless the person is about to become an in-law or spouse. It is dangerous to give "gifts" away because *your* game might suddenly fall apart while your opponent's game might suddenly start to improve.

What to Do When You Are Leading 5–0

How many times have you lost a set even though you had been leading 5-0, 5-1, or 5-2? If you play a lot of tennis, your answer is probably many times. Why is winning the sixth game so difficult?

> You let up on your game. You think you are almost there and do not concentrate as intensely.
>
> You change your style of play. If you were playing aggressively, you then switch to playing defensively. If your were playing defensively, you become very aggressive.
>
> You start to feel a little sorry for your opponent. His or her spouse is watching and you do have your opponent 5-0. "Why be greedy? Why not let him win just one more game?" you say. Suddenly the score is 5-7.
>
> You have never beaten this person and now you have him 5-1. Suddenly, you begin to have an identity crisis. You wonder, "Who am I? Who will I become if I beat him? I know who I am when he beats me, but this new person, this winner who is about to emerge, scares me a little."
>
> You fear that your relationship with your opponent is about to change. You had a safe and consistent relationship; usually he won and you lost. Your relationship off the court is also colored by the roles you play on the court. Suddenly, the 5-1 score seems to threaten the very foundations of your friendship. You feel that if you win that sixth game, nothing will be quite the same again.

To help you win the sixth game do the following:

> Even though you need only one more game, continue to concentrate with the same intensity. Make believe that you need twelve games rather than six to win a set of tennis. This technique will make the five games that you have already won seem like a very small accumulation of points. You will win the sixth game the same way you did the first five.
>
> Stay with the same style and game plan that got you the first five games. *Never change a winning game.*
>
> Do not feel sorry for anyone. There isn't any security in the 5-0 score. If you do not have six games, you have nothing.
>
> Be aware that your "loser" self-identity will try to sabotage the set. What you must do is trick the "loser" self. Tell yourself that just because you will win today doesn't mean that you will never go back to losing. Winning today is not killing the loser self. Tell yourself, "I am still a loser who will win just for today."
>
> Don't worry about losing that person as a friend or a spouse. You are still going to be the same two people who just happen to change roles for one day. For today you will be playing the part of the winner and your opponent the loser. If he can't handle the part for today, that's his problem.

chapter 18

Doubles

Now that it's time to discuss doubles, I've got some good news and some bad news to tell you. The good news is that in doubles we still use a tennis racket and a tennis ball. The bad news is that there the similarities end. Stroke selection, court positioning, and basic game strategies are different. Singles and doubles are just two different sports. The purpose of this chapter is to give you an in-depth look at the "game of doubles."

Doubles can be defined as a *team tennis experience within which each member assumes a strategically functional position which allows both teammates to have fun while receiving exercise*. Regardless of how primitive or advanced your game, this definition is valid.

A TEAM EXPERIENCE

While four people are supposedly playing a friendly *game*, the doubles court has the potential of becoming the loneliest, most pressured, and most painful environment around. Everyone is usually so worried about his own game or his partner's game that he forgets it's a *team* and not an individualized experience. Both partners should feel that having a great time together on the court is *more* important than winning. This "team experience" will enable each member to play the best tennis he is capable of. Only when each teammate does not feel personally threatened by his partner can this "team experience" be created. If one teammate fears that the other will remove love, respect, or approval when a mistake occurs, the team will never be able to create an energizing and synergistic "team experience." Try to remember that your partner is not purposely making errors.

There are two important elements in doubles play:

1. The doubles formation that the team uses, and

2. The agreed-upon "team reason" for playing doubles.

THE DOUBLES FORMATION THAT THE TEAM USES

Assuming that each teammate has an effective serve, ground stroke, volley, and overhead smash, the team has the option of selecting one of three doubles formations:

1. One player at net and one back at the baseline formation,

2. Two players back at the baseline formation, or

3. Two players at the net formation.

While all three formations will be discussed, the two players at the net formation will enable the team to play most offensively. This is the formation that you see professional tennis players using.

One Player at Net and One Back at the Baseline Formation

This is the most popular formation, but what is popular is not always functional.

> There is a huge hole in between the net player and the baseline player. An opposing net player can easily volley a ball into this vulnerable opening (see Diagram 18–1).
>
> If the server stays back after serving, the receiver of the serve has an easier time of placing short angular cross-court shots into the server's doubles alley or into the server's right side of his service box.
>
> Unless the teammate playing the net is an advanced volleyer, he will not get enough exercise because the ball will rarely come to him.
>
> The teammate playing the net feels more like a spectator and less like a participant. When the ball does finally come to him, he is more prone to make errors because he was emotionally and physically removed from prior shots.

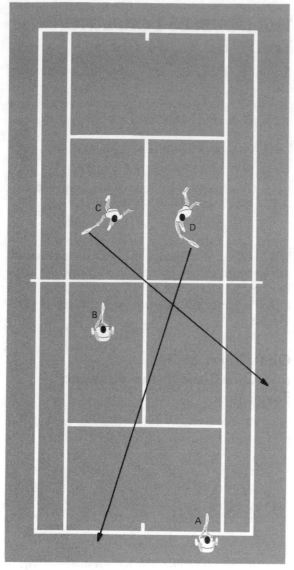

Diagram 18-1
With one player (B) at the net and the other player (A) back at the baseline formation, there are two vulnerable areas. D can volley a winner between A and B. By coming to the net, C can volley an angular cross-court winner.

Diagram 18-2
With both players (A and B), C and D can, given the opportunity, volley an angular cross-court winner.

Two Players Back at the Baseline Formation

Many players position themselves at net, yet never enjoy the experience. They see it as a painful but necessary part of doubles. Until your volley becomes pleasurable and efficient, why subject yourself to a painful and pressurized hour of tennis? Why not create a less threatening environment for yourself? You will find yourself playing more tennis when you are truly having fun. You can work on your volley in a safer environment until you feel a little more comfortable applying it in a pressurized atmosphere.

Although it looks elementary and unsophisticated, having both teammates staying back at the baseline area will enable the team to fulfill more of the doubles requirements than the previous formation (see Diagram 18–2a). The advantages of this formation are the following:

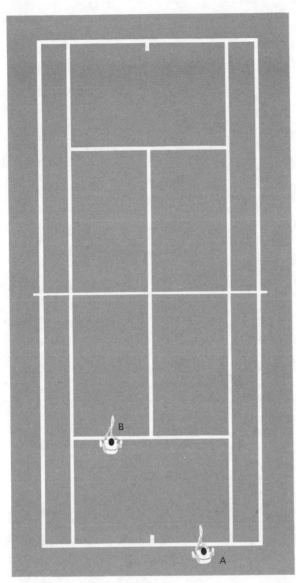

Diagram 18-3a
Two players at the net formation
before the point begins.

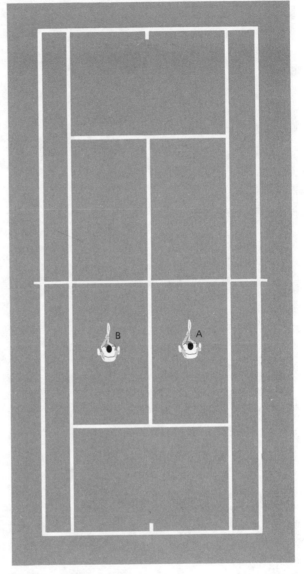

Diagram 18-3b
Soon after the point begins.

Your team is closing the most vulnerable hole in the middle of the court.

Both teammates are now able to use ground strokes. (Most players have better ground strokes than volleys.)

More of a team feeling can be experienced because both teammates are now closer together and can easily see one another.

The percentage of balls coming to each person is more likely to be 50 percent.

If both opponents choose to play the net, they will be forced to use two difficult strokes: volley and overhead smash.

Two Players at the Net Formation

The purpose of this formation is to have both players positioned at the net as soon as possible. (See Diagrams 18–3a and b.) Assuming

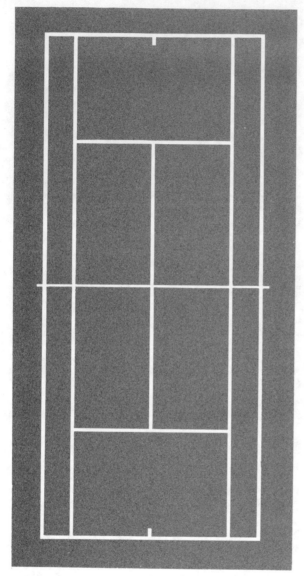

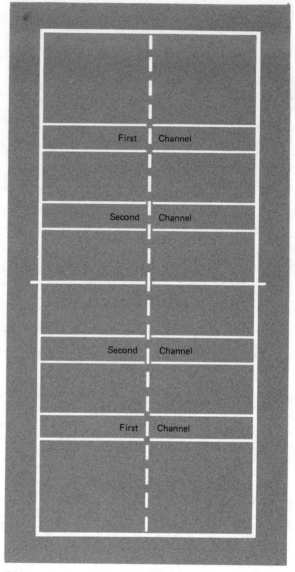

Diagram 18-4
(a) Actual tennis court,

(b) imaginary channeled tennis court,

that both teammates have an effective volley and overhead smash, this is the most offensive formation. The advantages of this formation are the following:

> The team's position at net leaves fewer vulnerable areas for the opponents to hit into.

> Both members of your team are more actively involved with each point.

Angular shots are easier to produce when at net than when at the baseline.

Many opponents will be intimidated when they see both members of your team playing the net.

When both teammates play the net, the opponents are forced to make more specific shots. Pressure is put on the opposing team to perform.

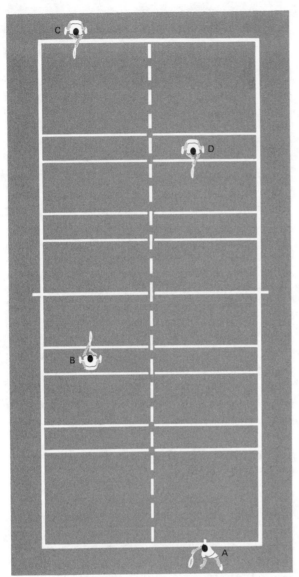

(c) channel positions when the point begins, and

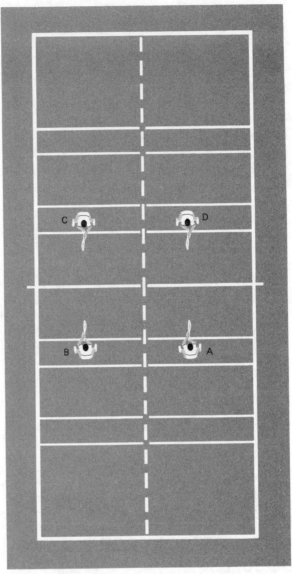

(d) channel positions soon after the point begins.

The disadvantages of this formation are the following:

> If any team member does not have an effective volley or overhead smash, he/she won't be able to take advantage of the offensive net position.

> Your team is vulnerable to the lob (a high arcing ball) because it can fly over both your heads.

The Channel Concept

Although the two players at net formation is the most competitive positioning on the doubles court, it requires a certain team choreography to enable the players to arrive at net as quickly and effectively as possible. The best way to do this is to use what I call The Channel Concept—a two part journey to the net. This method of getting into net formation is required because even world class athletes have a hard time running from baseline to net in one sprint. (See Diagrams 18–4a through d.)

Part one of the journey consists of the baseline player running up to the service line area of the court. The service line crosses the middle of the first channel. This is called the defensive volley channel because it is difficult to produce an offensive volley from this position. The player should enter this channel and assume a stationary ready alert position *before* his opponent contacts the ball.

After the player (or his partner) contacts the ball, part two of the journey begins. The player runs up to the net area (approximately ten feet away from it). This area forms a second channel (called the offensive volley channel). While in this channel it is easier to produce an offensive volley. Once again, the player should enter this channel and assume a stationary ready alert position *before* his opponent contacts the ball.

The positioning goal of both teams (assuming they both are using the Two Players at the Net Formation) is to have both teammates safely enter the second channel (an offensive volley channel) as soon as possible. (See Diagram 18–4d.)

THE AGREED-UPON "TEAM REASON" FOR PLAYING DOUBLES

Assuming that each teammate does *not* have an effective serve, ground stroke, volley, and overhead smash, then the selection of the doubles formation is determined by the "team's reason" for playing doubles.

The most popular "team reasons" for playing tennis are to have fun; to win, at almost any cost, even if one (or each) teammate is not enjoying the position he is playing; and to practice playing the offensive two players at net formation, even though it is not yet the team's most efficient or effective formation.

To Have Fun

If you are playing doubles just to have fun, then both you and your teammate should play positions that you are comfortable and relaxed playing. If you have any discomfort, tension, or fear while playing the net, then do not play this position. Stay back behind the baseline during the entire point. By practicing the volley in a non-competitive environment, you can become more comfortable and proficient with this stroke.

To Win

If both members of your team agree that you want to win, regardless of the method used, then the stronger member usually plays a disguised form of singles. This is accomplished by convincing the weaker player to wait near or in the doubles alley and very close to the net. While in this position, he or she is assured of only getting about three balls each hour. Now that the weaker player is removed from most of the action, the stronger player can play a very aggressive game either at the baseline or at the net. This formation is most heavily used when money, trophies, or egos are on the line.

To Practice Playing the Two Players at Net Formation

The most offensive team formation is created when both teammates come to net soon after the point begins. They might be using this formation even though their volleys and overheads might be weak and they might feel uncomfortable executing these strokes. This formation needs to be practiced many times before the teammates learn to enjoy the formation and to properly execute the necessary strokes.

The following diagrams show the sequence of moves and shots that allow each team to safely approach the second channel.

While all players want their eventual destination to be the second channel, they begin the point in the above positions. (See Diagram 18–5a.)

A must serve the ball from behind the baseline.

B can start in the second channel because a proficient serve should place the server's team in an offensive position.

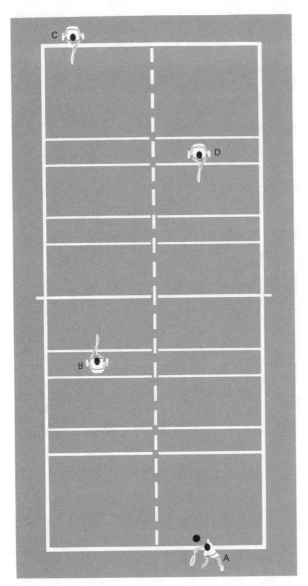

Diagram 18-5
(a) The beginning formation,

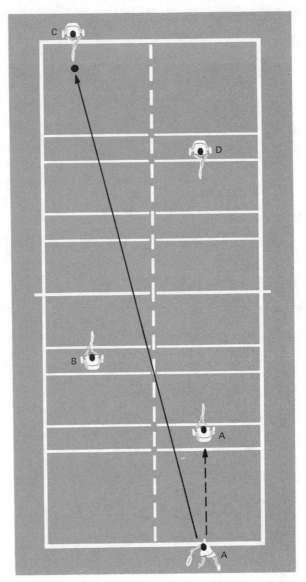

(b) the post-serve formation,

▬▬▶ = where a ball has just come from.
--▶ = where a player has just come from.

C must remain back to return A's serve.

D remains back in the first channel for reasons of safety:

1. Just in case C's service return is weak and directed at B, D does not want to be in the second channel, where he would have less time to prepare for B's return, and where he might get hurt;

2. Just in case B (the server's teammate) poaches,[1] D will have a little more time to react, and therefore a better chance to return his opponent's shot (because he is a little further away from the net).

After serving, A moves into the first channel just before receiver C contacts the ball. The

1. When a net player runs onto his teammate's side in order to volley the ball and his teammate is playing the baseline, his volleying action is referred to as a poach.

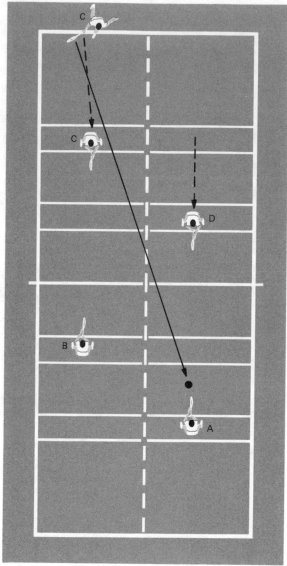

Diagram 18-5 (*cont.*)
(c) the post-service return,

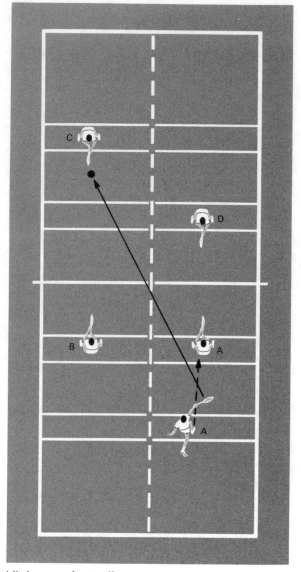

(d) the post-first volley,

server is the only player so far to change positions. (See Diagram 18–5b.)

Remember that whenever a player enters a channel, he/she should become stationary *before* the opponent contacts the ball.

After returning the serve back cross-court to A, C runs into the first channel. When D sees that C's service return has sufficient power and is directed back to A (out of B's reach) then D safely enters the second channel. D deter-

mines this by watching the ball *after* it has been contacted as it flies past him. (D should never watch his teammate C contact the ball, because he can make C nervous and he also stands a chance of getting hit in the eye with his teammate's ball.) (See Diagram 18–5c.)

Server A volleys the ball back cross-court to C and joins teammate B in the second channel. A and B are now both waiting to volley the ball from the second channel (the

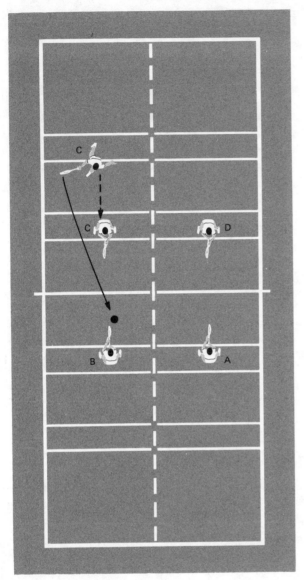

(e) the post-second volley, and

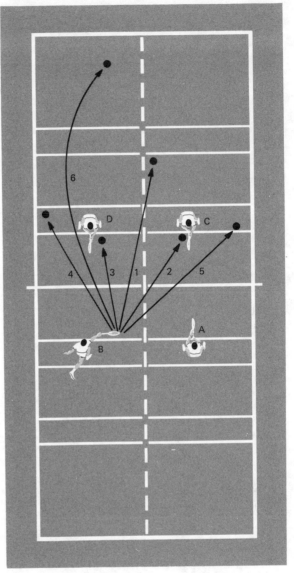

(f) the additional volleys.

offensive volley channel), while C is about to volley the ball from the first channel (the defensive volley channel). Because both members of the serving team AB have now arrived in the second channel, their team has the offensive volley advantage. (See Diagram 18–5d.)

C volleys the ball to B and moves into the second channel. The reason C volleys the ball to B is that B has not yet contacted the ball, and therefore might be mentally or physically re-

moved from the point ("dormant"). C, however, also has the option to volley the ball to A, in between A and B, or into B's doubles alley. (See Diagram 18–5e.)

Once all four players arrive in the second channel, each player has six directional options. (See Diagram 18–5f.)

1. To volley the ball down the middle of the opponent's court.

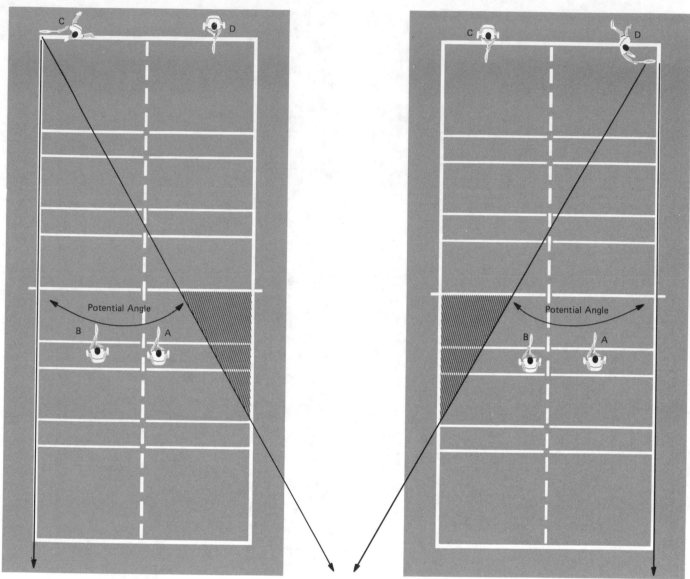

Diagram 18-6
Move in tandem to bisect
your opponent's potential angle.

2. To volley the ball to the dormant member.

3. To volley the ball back to the opponent who just sent him the ball.

4. To volley the ball into the left doubles alley.

5. To volley the ball into the right doubles alley.

6. To volley the ball over the opponent's head (a difficult and dangerous shot because your opponent might be able to hit an overhead smash into your mouth).

Note that all of B's returns except the lob should have low net clearance.

When both of your opponents are approaching or are already in the second channel, here are a few general rules to follow:

1. Direct the ball low over the net (except for the lob). Your goal should be to force

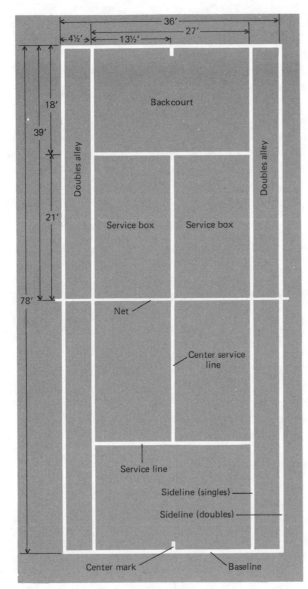

Diagram 18-7
Dimensions of a tennis court.

b. The net is lowest in the middle of the court.

c. A down the middle shot can confuse the teamwork of your opponents because sometimes neither one will know who should return the ball.

3. Direct the ball to the opponent further away from you (they are less likely to produce an offensive shot). When both opponents are an equal distance away from you, the ball should be directed toward the weaker player. If the opponents are the same distance from you and they have equal skills, direct the ball toward the player who was not involved in producing the previous shot. This is because the "dormant" player is less likely to be physically or mentally alert.

DOUBLES POSITIONING ONCE IN THE SECOND CHANNEL

Once you and your teammate join each other in the second channel, you should always move in tandem, as if connected by a rope. After contacting the ball, your team should move together toward the side of the court to which your ball was directed (see Diagram 18–6).

This tandem concept also applies when your opponent lobs. Whenever your team is in the second channel and your opponent successfully lobs over your head, you *both* should run back in tandem to the baseline area.[2] As soon as a ball lands shallow in your court, your team should run back in tandem into the second channel.

your opponents to contact the ball below the height of the net, making it more difficult for them to produce an offensive shot.

2. Direct the ball down the middle of the court more often than into the doubles alleys. There are three reasons for this:

a. Your opponents usually cover the alley, leaving the middle of the court less guarded.

2. Sometimes you might have to retrieve a ball that flies over your partner's head and lands on his side of the court. In such a case both teammates would switch sides as they both run back to the baseline area. Note that when you run back to the baseline, it is safer and faster to run sideways.

Conclusion

I once heard that after a stupendous Shakespearean performance, Sir Laurence Olivier came backstage in a fury. "What's the matter?" a fellow thesbian asked. "You just received twelve curtain calls. You were brilliant tonight."

"I know," he answered, "but why was I brilliant tonight and not every night?"

I can assure you that no matter how much you improve, you will never be fully satisfied with your tennis game. You will always be demanding greater excellence—just as Sir Laurence did.

Pleasure and precision are variables that constantly change. Your strokes will come and they will go, regardless of your level, and those "incredible days" can be just as fleeting as the night. In fact, the more you hold onto them, the sooner they will disappear.

What is important is not that those best days remain, but rather that you know how to recreate them when your game falls apart. When the electricity goes out in your house, you don't have to panic as long as you know where the circuit breaker box is. You should have the same detatched approach to your fleeting strokes.

The sensory and tennis imagery actions described in this book can be your circuit breakers during those moments when you have a pleasure and precision blackout. The more you practice the lessons contained here, the sooner you will be able to "switch on" your strokes, and the shorter your "off" periods will be. What once took weeks or months to fix can actually be corrected in seconds once you understand where all your circuit breakers are located.

Given the tenuous nature of your strokes, and the fact that each game or set can only have one winner, try to develop additional reasons for playing tennis. The expression "winning isn't everything" needs to be more than just a cliché if you're ever going to truly master *Ultimate Tennis*. Recreation means renewal and restoration to health. It does not mean being a tennis gladiator for the sake of fitness.

My hope is that the concept of Pleasure and Precision will open up an entirely new world for you—on and off the court. It will take time for you to fully accept the fact that pleasure is the foundation from which all precise actions are created—so be patient with yourself. Experiment with these concepts, particularly in pressure situations, until Pleasure and Precision are experiences, not ideas. Once you have felt the benefits of *Ultimate Tennis*, it is my firm belief that you will never want to return to a tense and uncomfortable game again.

Well, that's it for now, sports fans. Have fun.